GET THE
LOOK

GET THE
LOOK

EXTRAORDINARY
STYLE ON AN
ORDINARY
BUDGET

MARK HEYES

An Hachette UK Company
www.hachette.co.uk

First published in Great Britain in 2010 by
Hamlyn, a division of Octopus Publishing Group Ltd
Endeavour House, 189 Shaftesbury Avenue,
London, WC2H 8JG
www.octopusbooks.co.uk
www.octopusbooksusa.com

Distributed in the U.S. and Canada by Octopus Books USA:
c/o Hachette Book Group
237 Park Avenue
New York, NY 10017

Mark Heyes asserts the moral right to be identified
as the author of this work

ISBN 978-0-600-62159-1

Printed and bound in China

10 9 8 7 6 5 4 3 2 1

Contents

Ever since I can remember I have adored fashion. As a teenager I was obsessed with replicating the glamorous looks created by catwalk designers, the real thing being well out of my reach. In recent years duplicating a look has become ever easier, as styles permeate speedily down from the catwalk to appear as mass-produced garments in chain stores.

Introduction

These quick fashion fixes can be fantastic mood lifters, but fashion trends can change on a weekly basis, and trying to keep up is expensive and exhausting. Don't get me wrong—as a stylist who checks out dozens of shops every day of his life, I love a good "fashion must-have" purchase, but the mentality of disposable style can sometimes get out of hand.

Thankfully, certain looks are always on trend and simply never go out of fashion, and it's these particular designer looks that really interest me. This is where signature trends can play an essential role in every woman's wardrobe.

A great example of this could be the simple combination of a black V-neck, a crisp white shirt, some long pearls, and a black rose corsage. This outfit epitomizes

Chanel and all the label stands for—class, wealth, and Parisian glamour. The same can be said for a fitted blouse, a pencil skirt with a hint of lace, and some leopard-print shoes. It's an ensemble with Dolce & Gabbana written all over it.

The great news is that by searching the chain stores for the latest look-alikes from the runways, you can pick up these designer looks without breaking the bank. It's all about styling them up to give you not only a designer look, but also your own signature style.

The trick to pulling off a specific look is to find a version of it that suits

leopard heels à la D&G

CHANEL LOOK
"Simple yet effective."
Basic garments that ooze Parisian style.

you both physically and mentally. It's all very well looking great in an outfit, but if you don't have the confidence to leave the house in it, then it's not right for you. This book shows you ten designer looks that are all absolute classics, and for each of these ten looks you'll find five variations—something to suit everyone, no matter what your age, size, or shape.

You'll need to play your part in this fashion adventure, too. For starters, no matter what age you are, always keep up to date by reading the fashion magazines. My advice is buy one of the biggies at the beginning of each season (February and September). They'll usually include a catwalk guide that gives you a really understandable overview of the season's key looks. So take note and make fashion-wise purchases all season long. If you are more mature, you should still visit the younger shops. They tend to have better runway look-alikes, and a Balenciaga-esque bag on someone slightly more mature can look seriously authentic.

Take this opportunity to give your wardrobe a review. Start from the inside and check over your undies. Up to 70 percent of women wear the wrong bra size, and there really

isn't any excuse for that. Most department stores have a free bra-fitting service, and the staff will usually be very knowledgeable about styles. This is important because it's not just the size that matters—the shape can be vital, too. Once you've found a great bra, the difference you'll feel in your posture and confidence will astound you. Turn to my Ultimate Underwear guide on page 42 for some more help with choosing the right items to go under your new look outfits.

Besides trawling the shops, rummage through the back of your closet and see what's actually there. Often you'll find a top, skirt, or dress that you've forgotten about. Try reworking it with some of your new purchases and create a this-season treasure.

When you are out shopping, step outside your comfort zone and buy a little something you never usually would. It's all too easy to wear the same old styles time and time again, even to the extent of buying new items that you already have lurking in your closet. It doesn't have to be an expensive purchase—colored or lacy tights, a waist belt, or a brightly colored bag can really give a style lift and expand your fashion horizons.

CONFIDENCE
Remember, the outfit shouldn't wear you. You should wear the outfit and feel sensational!

belt

You'll find that a great asset for the aspiring, but budget-conscious, fashionista is a tailor. We're not talking *haute couture*, just a local tailor—your dry cleaner may well know one or even employ one. Make friends with this tailor—he or she will be able to work wonders by tweaking your chain store purchases to fit you perfectly and so give your outfits a real designer look.

Even when you're buying chain store garments, don't be disposable with your fashion —look after it. Even the most inexpensive garments come with spare buttons, so do yourself a favor and keep all spare buttons in one place. A missing button can make or break an outfit. In the same vein, always carry an emergency kit—safety pins, wipes, toupee tape, and a prethreaded needle are essential. You never know when disaster may strike, and what friends you'll make when there's a ripped seam on the dance floor.

Try getting into the habit of treating yourself a bit. Get that "just walked out of the salon" look every week by getting a good old-fashioned blow-dry. It needn't cost you a fortune—try either local salons or speedy haircut stores—and you'll feel glossy and fabulous for days on end. Go to a big department store and take full advantage of all those bored makeup artists standing around in the cosmetics department. Just limit yourself to the price of a lipstick and get some professional help with a new makeup look. Then go home and take some snaps and make some notes so you remember how the look was achieved, and try re-creating it with products you already have, plus your new lipstick!

Instead of spending the evening in front of the TV, try pampering yourself. Run a bath, light a few candles, shape your nails, cleanse, tone, moisturize, and go to bed early feeling utterly gorgeous and ready for a great new day. These treats will help boost your confidence, and the more confident you are, the better you look. With that in mind, the next time you're in a fitting room and the lady next to you looks fabulous, tell her so. When you make somebody feel great, you'll feel great, too.

I really hope that in the pages of this book you'll find inspiration for a whole new fashion you. There's a huge amount to choose from, with extra hints and tips to help start you off with your newfound image. And my gorgeous, lovely models are all shapes, ages, and sizes, proving that each and every one of you can get the look.

Mark Heyes

FRENCH CLASSIC

The style I'm calling French Classic is embodied by the phenomenon of French fashion that is Chanel. Ever since its 1910 creation by Gabrielle "Coco" Chanel, the fashion house's designs have offered that elusive quality we call "chic" and have been adored by the rich, the famous, and the fashionista alike.

Get the look

Chanel's true claim to fame is arguably the creation of what we lovingly call the LBD (little black dress). It's now a wardrobe staple for most women and can be a fabulous asset for figures of any age, shape, or size. The Chanel we know and love today is fronted by the king, the don, the genius of fashion that is Mr. Karl Lagerfeld. He's been at the helm of Chanel since 1983, and under his talented eye the design house is still as innovative and chic as when Coco first put pen to paper and needle to thread. Mr. Lagerfeld has updated classic Chanel styles for the 21st century, allowing us to wear bouclé jackets with denims, oversized pearls with transparent white shirts, and big, bold glasses with the beloved double C emblazoned on the sides.

Whether it be fashion, perfume, or makeup that you associate with Chanel, there are three colors that sum up the French Classic style. The combination of black, gold, and cream oozes expensive simplicity and is, thankfully, supereasy to replicate.

LILY ALLEN
Although every piece worn in this ensemble is as classic as can be, the combination of the quilted bag, the long-line gold necklace, the shorter-length sheath, and those opaque tights screams youthfulness with a serious fashion edge. It's no wonder she's a muse for Mr. Lagerfeld.

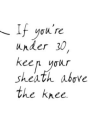

If you're under 30, keep your sheath above the knee.

PENELOPE CRUZ
This outfit is sophisticated, glamorous, yet understated all at the same time. The ultra-versatile Chanel jacket can be teamed with so many wardrobe staples, and the black wide-leg pants are always a fabulously flattering choice.

CLAUDIA SCHIFFER
Even though Claudia's dressed in a classic Chanel suit, it hasn't aged her in the slightest. Whether you're a wealthy, mature, chic Parisian lady or a twenty-something fashion starlet, this is absolute proof that the French Classic style is wardrobe-worthy for all generations.

Ultra-versatile jacket.

A classic she'll wear and wear again.

Loving the logo.

This is as timeless as it gets—you can't beat a classic sheath and a matching Chanel-style jacket. It doesn't matter what age, shape, or size you are, this look is wearable, flattering, and seriously sleek. A simple sheath that's slightly fitted around the waist is perfect if you're aged 40 or above. It will nip you in at the waist while skimming and minimizing the hips.

True
CLASSIC

Try and find a lined sheath; the lining will cling to your body while the outer layer of fabric keeps that silhouette clean, lean, and fabulous. Don't be scared of mixing in some pattern here. The bold, stylized rose design is another great trick for attracting eyes away from areas you'd rather they didn't linger on.

Attention to detail is key for this look: a darker edge on the collar and cuffs of the jacket oozes Chanel style. When you do get your hands on one of these classics, it'll be a wardrobe friend for life.

Remember that less is more when we're talking about flesh for this look, so make sure your neckline is relatively high and that the dress hem hits the knee, guaranteeing that you look demure at all times.

classic pearls

If you are going to splurge on something special, then a strand of honest-to-goodness real pearls is the finest neck candy a woman can own. They can be styled with an LBD outfit, a black turtleneck, or even a basic T-shirt to make a chain store outfit look outrageously couture.

padded bag

The IT bag of all IT bags is Chanel's ever-classic 2.55—duplicated by many chain stores, so you can easily find one. Your bag has to be padded with a diagonal diamond stitch; add a leather-woven chain and try a Union Jack motif for a fashion forward edge.

This look has to be worn with a high heel, and there's nothing more chic than a monochrome stiletto. It instantly adds glamour and is a great way of making large feet look smaller. Always look for a platform sole; you get the height without the blisters and pain!

monochrome heels

"Three-quarter-length sleeves are great for longer arms"

As you can see, the French Classic look doesn't always have to be prim and proper; it can be as youthful and fun as an MTV beach party. The combination of a cropped tweed jacket and skinny denims in a pale tone is very Chanel prêt-à-porter.

Contemporary
CLASSIC

With this look it's all about playing around with proportions and not taking it too seriously. The tweed jacket is the anchor piece, but go for a cream, flesh, or pale blue color. Make sure it's cropped to the hip, and if you're feeling creative, try sewing pearls or fringing on the edges.

Underneath, wear a long tank top that just covers your derriere, and then overload those pearl strands.

For maximum style points, combine different-sized pearls with different-length strands—you can pick up strings of these in chain stores for next to nothing. To complete the catwalk vibe, make sure some strands are long enough to reach your waist.

For the ultimate skinny denims, make sure that in bare feet the length hits the bottom of your heel, and always go for the tightest pair you can handle. Remember that denims don't shrink anymore; the Lycra® content in the denim actually makes them bigger over a very short period of time.

To add to the authentic Chanel glamour, always keep a watchful eye out for fringed edges on a jacket. This signature style feature will have even the chicest Parisian thinking your jacket cost a fortune.

An oversized quilted bag still has all the elegance of its more petite sister, but is so much more youthful and practical. Black versions can sometimes be a bit harsh, so try gray, navy, or cream for ultimate sophistication.

two-tone flats

This is one of the few times you'll see me style up an outfit with a pair of flats (male stylists can be notoriously mean to a girl's feet). A pair of quilted two-tone flats is chic, elegant, and comfy—three words you rarely see together.

fringed edging

big quilted bag

"A cropped tweed jacket and skinny denims are youthful, fun Chanel"

"A black top and skirt create extra length"

Chanel-inspired chic can look just as elegant on a petite lady as on a gazelle-like supermodel, as long as you obey a few rules. It's all about elongating your shape, so a classic cropped jacket may look great on the hanger, but it's a definite no-no if you're on the shorter side.

Classic
PETITE

I know only too well that many petite ranges leave a lot to be desired and miss out on great trends. On the other hand, classic shapes that never go out of fashion are much easier to come by. These items may not have you reaching for your purse at first glance, but when styled and accessorized correctly, it's a completely different story.

A black pencil skirt that hits the top of the knee is a must-have purchase for any petite woman.

To create extra length, go for a black top; this will give the illusion of a taller, more svelte silhouette.

Never go for oversized items when it comes to accessories. A large clutch will make you look like a five-year-old who's borrowed her mother's handbag, and big glasses can look slightly flylike. The same principle applies to the all-important pearls—keep them small and always above the bust. Be cautious of large collars and cuffs, too.

A black rose is another of Chanel's signature motifs. Combine a stylized rose corsage with a classic strand of pearls, or wear it solo on a tweed jacket; either way it looks a million Euro.

sunglasses

This is the one and only time I permit a logo to be as gratuitous as humanly possible. Let the big CCs do the talking in crystal, gold, or even a chic and simple monochrome colorway.

When it comes to heels, a simple pair of black stilettos is the only partner for this classic, uncomplicated outfit. They are an essential part of any capsule wardrobe and will be worn and worn again.

rose corsage

classic heels

The important thing for curvaceous ladies to remember is that one solid color—especially when it's black—is superflattering, elongating, and seriously slimming. Although a cropped jacket may ring alarm bells because it shows off your derriere, there are tricks of the trade that can keep an expensive vibe and accentuate your best features.

Classic
CURVES

The jacket can't be too boxy and needs a small amount of shapely tailoring to nip you in at the waist and show off those womanly curves. A simple black top layered underneath will allow the jacket fronts to create two lines that run down the body, making you look instantly slimmer.

An essential part of this look is a good-quality pair of black, wide-leg pants. These great figure fixers elongate your shape still further. A low-slung chain belt can help extend this elongation. The diagonal line it creates offsets any widening horizontal lines the jacket or top make. Oversized pearls and an oversized bag finish off the look, and help draw the eye away from any problem areas.

If you see a low-slung woven chain belt, then it's happy days all around. If you're not so lucky, it's time to get creative. Buy a chain belt and weave through a length of plastic leather-look ribbon—let the style do the talking.

chain belt

oversized handbag

Playing around with proportions is a fabulous trick for looking smaller than you actually are. Bauble-sized pearls focus attention to your top half, besides being extremely fashion savvy.

oversized pearls

Go for a light-colored bag to break up the outfit without breaking up your svelte appearance. Again, the large dimensions make you look smaller than you are, and when you add a padded diagonal stitch pattern, you'll have serious fashionista style with a distinctive air of Chanel. Plus, you can fit your life in a supersized bag!

"One solid color is seriously slimming"

"An elegant
sheath is
tasteful and
demure"

A sheath dress is perfect for day or evening, from office to bar, or even for more formal events. Although Chanel may be known for its chic, tailored jackets, an elegant sheath on its own (and on the right figure) is tasteful and demure. Choose cream rather than black for extra va-va-voom. Accessorizing with black adds depth and keeps within the color palette of the French Classic style.

Classic OCCASIONS

An LCD (little cream dress) won't be as slimming as an LBD, but some trusty hold-in underwear and a cream slip will smooth away any lumps and bumps. It's perfectly acceptable to show both arms and legs with this look, but NEVER legs above the knee.

A hair accessory always adds an air of sophistication. Try an oversized black silk rose: put it toward the front of your hair to achieve true catwalk glamour.

When it comes to footwear there are no Chanel-esque flats here—high heels are a must. Keep it simple and match with a monochrome shoe. As for the bag, experiment with a vintage-style hard-cased bag; it may not be the most practical choice, but that retro touch will make you top the trend radar.

CHANGE THE LOOK

To convert your Classic Occasions look into a work look, simply dispense with the rose in your hair, but keep your oversized bracelet. Slip on a one-button suit jacket, and add a narrow black leather belt and an over-the-shoulder black bag.

The best way to manage any wardrobe is to have a collection of essential basic items that can be dressed up or dressed down. All of these must-have pieces should be in a solid color and should mix and match with each other. This allows key fashion items to be slotted straight in, so there should be no more random fashion purchases that stay at the back of your closet. Once you get capsule wardrobe savvy, you'll never look back. Here are some fashion investments you won't regret.

CAPSULE WARDROBE

LBD (LITTLE BLACK DRESS) AND PENCIL SKIRT
Think classic and flattering to your body shape. Make the dress Roland Mouret Galaxy-esque if you're curvy, empire-line if you have a fuller figure, body-conscious if you're young and slim, or a simple wrap style if you're more mature. Make sure a skirt hem hits either the top of the knee or the center of the knee. Shorter looks tacky, longer looks frumpy.

BLACK ONE-BUTTON JACKET
Just watch as the sleek, tailored lines create a waist, even if you didn't think you had one. Team the jacket with your black pencil skirt for work or with denims and a T-shirt for weekend casual.

WIDE-LEG PANTS
These skim butts, lengthen legs, and create the same width at the bottom of your leg as there is at the top to give a column effect that visually melts away the pounds: invest in black, gray, and cream pairs for year-round flattery.

T-SHIRTS THAT SUIT YOUR SHAPE
If you're small in the bust department a turtle- or crew-neck T-shirt is best for you, because the high neckline accentuates what you have. Bigger-busted ladies should go for either a deep V-neck or a low-cut scoop neck.

JEANS IN BLUE AND BLACK
It's easier said than done to find the perfect pair of denims. A pair of skinny and a pair of boot-cut jeans in each color will serve all your denim needs.

Other great basic items include a fitted white shirt, black tights in 40 and 80 denier, a selection of tank tops, V-neck sweaters (and turtleneck sweaters if you have a small or average-size bust), and black patent pumps.

Keep a fitted bright white shirt..

Have a perfect selection of t-shirts and vests for your shape.

The must-have LBD.

Buy leggings, 40- and 80-denier tights, and black high heels.

Tailored wide-leg pants, boot-cut and skinny jeans are essential.

Dolce & Gabbana

SUPERBLY SEXY

Since Domenico Dolce and Stefano Gabbana started their label in 1986, their designs have become the essence of Italian fashion and glamour. The typical Italian woman isn't scared to show her sensuality, and the clothes they've designed do just that, celebrating the superbly sexy female form.

Get the look

classic animal print.

The inimitable signature Dolce & Gabbana look starts with the body-conscious dress, and remember that curves are a bonus here! It's got to be tight and worn with confidence (big hold-in undies can really help). The length is usually to the knee, which means it tends to be your cleavage that's on display. You know the saying: bosom or legs, it's got to be one OR the other.

Colorwise the palette tends to lean to supersexy black, with some show-stopping metallics thrown in for good measure. The other hue the company is most famous for is the color of love—red. Once you mix in some animal print, whether it be leopard, tiger, snake, or even zebra, the D&G look is almost complete.

The finishing touches have to be some of those famous accessories: a corset-style waist belt, a simple clutch bag, a hint of lace underwear, sickeningly high stilettos, vampy red lips, and an attitude to die for.

SCARLETT JOHANSSON

If you're going to do animal print, then do it in style. This gorgeous coat makes even the dullest of outfits spring to life. Scarlett really pulls off this look, which will be flattering on other figure shapes, too. The self-colored coat belt cinches in your waist, even if you don't think you have one.

VICTORIA BECKHAM

This outfit is as sexy as it gets. The skinny cut of the leather trousers keeps it ultramodern without even a hint of the 80s, and the solid black adds an air of sophistication and true Italian glamour. It's a classic look that's still got a high-fashion edge.

Superskinny and supersexy.

Classic tight, lacy corset dress.

Knee-length cut.

KYLIE MINOGUE

The body-con dress encapsulates how D&G feel a woman should dress, and with sex appeal, sass, and confidence, Kylie certainly does them proud here. The cut is second to none and simply oozes class, making Kylie look every bit the sex goddess and never cheap or tacky.

DOLCE & GABBANA 31

You need to bite the bullet on this one and work with your curves rather than against them. A shapely figure will improve this look and will turn heads, too. Let's begin with a piece of tailoring: a one-button jacket will instantly create a waist, giving you hourglass lines that will look fabulous whether you're a size 6 or size 16.

Sleek and SEXY

Make sure the jacket's not too cropped —the perfect length hits you halfway down your derriere. This keeps things looking sexy and seriously flattering.

Underneath the jacket lies Dolce's signature red color and this will certainly make you stand out from the crowd. Work from the inside out here with some well-structured hold-in undies and a supportive, yet sublimely sexy, bra. Once you're pushed and pulled in all the right places, a body-con dress is the only way forward. The rule of thumb is that the more you spend, the thicker the fabric and the more flattering the contour. Make sure the fabric has a good amount of stretch as this will act like another layer of hold-in panties.

Always remember that the dress hem should hit just on the knee. A higher hem says trashy rather than fashionista.

lace bra

Find a bra with a lace trim and make sure it shows! This was a trend D&G pioneered many years ago, and it is still as sexy and sassy now as it was then.

Dolce's signature heels are pointy and as high as can be, perfect for a more voluptuous figure. If, on the other hand, these fill you with horror, not-so-high satin pumps are a wardrobe staple and an investment you'll never regret.

versatile satin heels

rhinestone button

Dolce & Gabbana's look is all about glitz and glamour. By adding bits of bling, you can change an everyday blazer into a couture must-have. Simply replace the existing button with a sparkling find from the notions department.

"Bite the bullet and work with your curves"

Dolce & Gabbana like to use a masculine silhouette in the creation of an ultrafeminine look. This combination of a crisp black shirt and suit jacket teamed with leather pants and a leopard-print bra is just dynamite! The jacket should be tailored to a perfect fit, so find a bargain blazer and take it to a tailor. This costs very little compared to the price of a Dolce suit jacket.

Sexy

TAILORING

Underneath the black shirt lies the all-important leopard-print bra. Don't worry, you don't need to show enough to get arrested; just a subtle glimpse of leopard will get you noticed for all the right reasons. The key to this version of the Superbly Sexy look are the leather pants. Make sure they're skinny-cut—NEVER boot-cut—and as tight as humanly possible (breathing isn't essential for this look). Even a slight flare will just scream 1992, and that's not the look you're going for. Take note, there are some harsh rules when it comes to leather pants. If you wore them the first time around—or even wanted to wear them the first time around—you simply can't go there again: the age limit lies at 35 and below.

structured shirt

Although there is mixed-gender feel to this style, you don't want to look like you've borrowed your boyfriend's shirt. Keep it structured and fitted with a high collar and with three buttons open for the optimum Dolce look. Remember, you can revive black cotton shirts with a simple redye in the washing machine for that just-bought look.

With such a supersexy look created by the clothes alone, less is more when it comes to jewelry, so just go for one key piece. An oversized statement cocktail ring is that winning combo of inexpensive and ultra-glamorous.

cocktail ring

Animal-print heels are a great way to bring that Dolce trend to any outfit. They finish this look off fabulously, but even with black jeans and a black tank top these cuties ooze Italian glamour and style.

leopard heels

"A subtle glimpse of leopard is all you need"

"Keep it tailored and high-waisted to help create those curves"

This is one of the sexiest looks you can go for, and there's no denying that it may take an extra glass of wine and a gaggle of friends for you to step out with confidence. As you can see, it doesn't leave much to the imagination so if you're a smaller-dress-sized, petite lady, this is *the* look for you.

Sexy and SHAPELY

When it comes to corsetry, the smaller your bust the better, so if you are well endowed this might not be the look for you. A tailored jacket over the top can help, but do try before you buy. If you're lucky enough to be petite all over, then an animal-print skirt is a real must-have. Keep it tailored and high-waisted to help create those curves. However, try and find a print that doesn't have a diagonal stripe, such as leopard or snake. If you go for tiger or zebra, this can seriously widen your lower half. Look for a stripe that runs vertically on the body for the most flattering result.

Once again, the simpler the better when it comes to accessories: black platform heels add those much-needed extra inches, while a jet-black bangle seals the deal.

corset

Dolce & Gabbana is famed for its beautiful corsetry, but styles have changed from the traditional corset that we all knew and loved. Try to avoid the boned, laced-up, Elizabethan-esque numbers and go for shaped cups and simple lines instead. A true stylist's tip is to head to a good lingerie department and try underwear as outerwear.

lace underskirt

metallic belt

A metallic waist belt adds Italian glamour to any outfit, as well as giving the illusion of a waist and the appearance of curves, no matter what your age, shape, or size.

An inch of lace peeking out from under your hem adds an extra Dolce dimension to an animal-print skirt. It can be an actual underskirt, or a piece of lace sewn to the inside hem to give even the dullest of outfits that superbly sexy edge.

The strapy LBD is a chic, understated canvas to do whatever you wish with. A beautifully made one exudes elegance and wealth and is just perfect for an intimate dinner or a fabulous party. From a practical point of view, a strapless, hold-in bodysuit underneath will always give you the extra confidence it takes to wear this body-hugging piece.

Sexy and STRAPPY

A gain, it is imperative that the dress length is correct: under no circumstances should it EVER be above the knee. Part of what Italian glamour and the Superbly Sexy look is all about is the clashing of two different themes, and this combination of lace and snakeskin is a gorgeous marriage. The key to making this mismatched look work is to have one item that relates to one other. Here, the bolero matches the bag, while the belt and shoes make a seriously hot combo. What's best is that all these fashion pieces can be worked individually into your existing wardrobe, creating different fashion masterpieces.

Because the upper arms are covered, this look is both ageless and timeless. Just make sure you team it with a good blow-dry, some killer red lips, and an air of confidence.

If you don't have the confidence to pull off the underwear as outerwear look, a lace bag gives any outfit a sexy edge. Here it ties in beautifully with the bolero and adds another dimension to this mismatched, sexy style.

bolero

Boleros don't have to be dowdy. Go for one in sexy lace to show just enough flesh without feeling self-conscious about your upper arms. Make sure you keep it short and sharp at all times; a lace cardigan, although more readily available, will age this outfit in an instant.

snakeskin belt

A waistband gives a helping hand in the waist department. Accentuate your waist even further by cinching it in with a waist belt in a paler colorway.

lace bag

"Combine
lace and
snakeskin for
a gorgeous
marriage"

"A faux-fur collar gives a basic coat an extra dimension"

This is a strong, self-assured, fashion-editor look that at first impression may scare the living daylights out of you. In fact, each individual piece is incredibly flattering, and when styled together they can work wonders on your figure. All eyes are on the coat here, and a tailored trench coat will be any girl's best friend. The lines of this piece will naturally slim the waist and skim over problem areas, elongating your figure.

Sexy
SILHOUETTE

Use a gold belt on the coat instead of its existing self-colored belt for an instant injection of glamour and wealth. The flare at the bottom detracts attention from your derriere.

A faux-fur collar gives a basic coat an extra dimension; simply attach it for the evening and detach it in the day.

Adding black wide-leg pants that echo the flare of the coat emphasizes the elegant, elongated shape. The combination of these two key pieces is one of fashion's most fabulous partnerships.

To give the outfit added pizzazz, go for animal print heels and an oversized gold bag.

CHANGE THE LOOK
Change this "front row of the catwalk" look to an everyday, but still superstylish, outfit by ditching the fur collar and reverting to the self-colored belt that came with the coat. Keep it supersimple underneath, with dark indigo denims and a black shirt.

DOLCE & GABBANA   **41**

Find the hottest hold-ins, the best body enhancers, and the ultimate bra for your perfect LBD. Before you just go ahead and buy, consider going for a fitting. Over 70 percent of women wear the wrong size bra, and getting the right size—and the right shape—for you is one of the quickest and easiest ways to boost your confidence and give yourself a makeover from the inside out. Here's the underwear you'll need to match different dress styles.

ULTIMATE UNDERWEAR

STRAPLESS DRESS

A strapless dress will always wow the crowds but can prove problematic in the bosom department. If you're on the larger side, go for a well-structured minimizing strapless bra (it may be worthwhile being properly fitted for this specialized bra). If you're not well-endowed, get a gel-filled strapless number. These are amazing at creating cleavage when you never thought such a thing possible.

HALTER-NECK DRESS

Don't even think about going braless! Your dress may look perfectly decent in front of the mirror at home, but a couple of glasses of bubbly and some dance steps can create havoc. Buy a multiway bra that will keep you in check without anyone knowing it's there. This is a good underwear investment, because the changeable straps allow you to wear it with other dresses, too.

BIAS-CUT DRESS

We all know the danger of slinky fabric dresses—they look beautiful on the hanger but can show too much lumpage and bumpage on you. Thankfully, there's a huge range of efficient tummy and thigh controllers out there. Make sure you buy one that's smooth and seamless; underwear lines or decorative detailing are a definite no-no with a bias cut.

PLUNGING NECKLINE

Keep plunging necklines looking classy by getting your hands on a matching plunging bra. Bras with a clear middle section work fantastically, giving maximum support and maximum security, and no one will even know it's there.

BODY-CON DRESS

These dresses clearly show the contours of your body, so create a smooth sihouette with an all-in-one butt-lifting, tummy-tucking, bust-enhancing bodysuit; separates can produce an unsightly bulge.

Strapless dress: hook your
bra on its tightest setting
for added security.

Plunging neckline:
slacken the bra straps
and insert some
cleavage-enhancing gels.

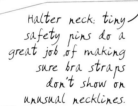

Halter neck: tiny
safety pins do a
great job of making
sure bra straps
don't show on
unusual necklines.

Bias-cut dress: the
seamless quality of
this longer-line bra
works perfectly with
hold-in underpants
to hide all lumps
and bumps.

Versace

BRIGHT AND BOLD

Versace's style is famously and fabulously glamorous, bright, bold, and undeniably sexy. Since its creation in 1978, the Versace fashion house has epitomized the dazzling allure of the fashion world, with all its whims and wonders.

Get the look

Plunging neckline.

It was Gianni himself who created the phenomenon that is "the supermodel," the girls who were so in demand in the 90s that they supposedly wouldn't get out of bed for less than $10,000. Fashion-wise, Versace was a pioneer in the use of bold color and had us loudly and proudly wearing cobalt blues, tangerine oranges, and superbright yellows.

When Gianni was murdered in 1997 everyone believed that the label would die with him. Instead, his sister Donatella took over as head designer and was greeted by a mixture of reactions. More than ten years down the line, Donatella has certainly proved herself to be a credible leader of Italian glamour and style with the Versace brand still a global influence on fashion.

The mass of bold color we saw in the 90s has been scaled down, but still features in many of Donatella's designs. One theme that very much remains is the indisputable feel of wealth and glamour, demonstrated through a clever use of metallics, clean crisp lines, figure-enhancing cuts, and supersexy silhouettes.

HALLE BERRY

The cobalt blue of Halle's dress works amazingly with her skin tone, and this intense color is classic Versace style. Add a plunging neckline to the mix and Italian fashion magic really starts to happen. This look isn't for the fainthearted, but it's sensual and still incredibly sophisticated.

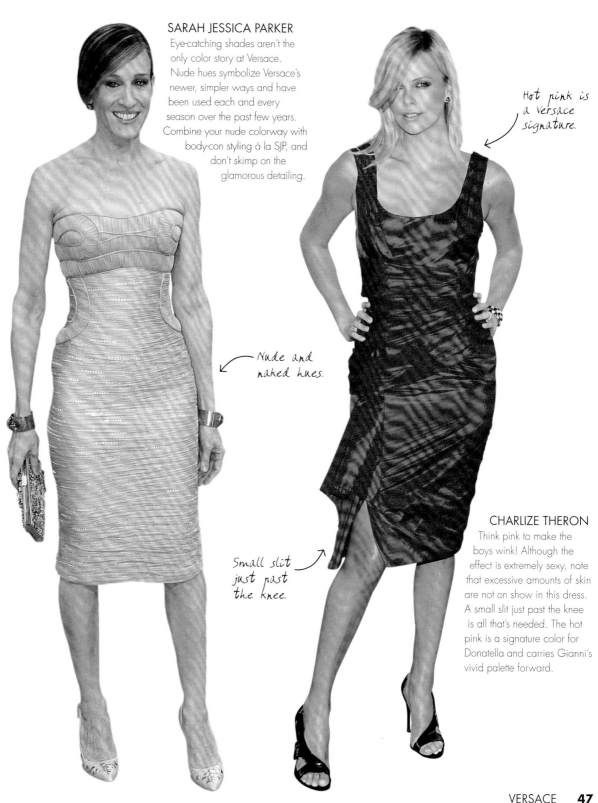

SARAH JESSICA PARKER
Eye-catching shades aren't the only color story at Versace. Nude hues symbolize Versace's newer, simpler ways and have been used each and every season over the past few years. Combine your nude colorway with body-con styling à la SJP, and don't skimp on the glamorous detailing.

Hot pink is a Versace signature.

Nude and naked hues.

Small slit just past the knee.

CHARLIZE THERON
Think pink to make the boys wink! Although the effect is extremely sexy, note that excessive amounts of skin are not on show in this dress. A small slit just past the knee is all that's needed. The hot pink is a signature color for Donatella and carries Gianni's vivid palette forward.

VERSACE **47**

This classic combination of white and cream is the epitome of wealth and sophistication. It may not be the most practical of outfits, but on the right occasion it's a winning mix. You may need a bit of confidence to pull it off, but it's a superflattering and glamorously chic look that is perfect for any age.

Summer BRIGHT

A white high-collared shirt is quintessentially Versace. Layer the shirt with a fabulous cream-colored suit jacket. The natural lines of a tailored jacket are always slimming and sleek, and going for metallic-finish linen adds to the luxurious feel.

Well-cut boot-cut denims will always give you an extra edge of confidence, even when wearing such light colors. They are fantastic at balancing out butts and hips and really will make your legs look longer. The combination of a white shirt and linen jacket leans toward the spring/summer season, but you can easily give this look a fall/winter twist by replacing the shirt with a sleek turtleneck and the linen jacket with a tailored leather number.

tan shoes

A pair of tan leather shoes will be a purchase you'll never regret. They can be dressed with black, brown, navy—in fact just about any color you can think of. Their neutral tone makes them a real wardrobe staple and invaluable when you're on vacation.

retro bag

The magic combination of tan, white, and gold is classic Versace through and through. The luxurious feel of the colors and slightly retro edge to this bag conjures up images of sipping vermouth on the Italian Riviera.

Go for an oversized pair of sunnies and wear them with style. Get the largest pair you can and never take them off—just push them up to sit on top of your head. The fake tortoiseshell frames are great because they work with everything.

tortoiseshell sunglasses

"For fall, try a turtleneck and tailored leather jacket"

Versace dresses aren't just about body-conscious silhouettes; many of the shapes sent down Donatella's runway are quite simple in style, so a basic-shaped, slightly oversized dress that's obviously cut to perfection will look just right. A good shift dress should show either cleavage or legs, not both at the same time.

Bright
WHITE

This chic and beautiful version draws attention to the legs. To contrast perfectly with the glowing white of the dress, you've got to have good skin color. If you are on the paler side, now is the time to get the fake stuff out. If you're doing it yourself, then exfoliate, moisturize, and apply the tan wearing soft cotton gloves. The aerosol versions are amazing when done professionally but can be disastrous on legs when done yourself. So either get to a salon, or get rubbing and buffing!

The key to this outfit is to avoid true color altogether and go for all white with a luxury gold accent. To add to your golden skin shimmer, accessorize with some stacked gold bangles on one wrist and finish off the look with some gold-rimmed, oversized sunglasses for a fashionista edge.

gold hoops

These offer inexpensive and effective instant glamour to even the most basic of outfits. Make sure your hoops are 1½–2 in. (4–5 cm) across. Any bigger can look trashy; any smaller will have no effect whatsoever.

A high-shine, gold leather bag is totally Versace, and if it has an embossed texture on the surface, so much the better. Try and get a clutch version for that superstar feel.

gold bag

gold shoes

Vertiginous stiletto heels have been a signature shoe style for many seasons in Versace's shows. Once you find the right shoes, you'll find that the gold color can be brought in to glam up any outfit—the ultimate in sophistication.

"For impact, go for white with a gold accent"

"This outfit should be fun, vivacious, and not taken too seriously"

Vibrant yellows and Versace go hand in hand, but this combination of such a loud color and a flesh-revealing garment certainly takes a bit of courage to pull off with style. The strapless cocktail dress should really be quite structured, and a heavy satin fabric will help get the look just right.

Color BRIGHTS

Flimsier fabrics on this kind of dress can look cheap and nasty and will cling to just about everything, but not in a good way. The thicker fabric can work really well at disguising a tiny tummy, but I've got to be honest here, you really need to be on the slimmer side to get away with this version of Bright and Bold.

Create yourself a subtle cleavage. If you naturally have one, you'll just need a good bra; if not, a gel-filled strapless bra will do the job. If you are well endowed go for a strappy version.

To introduce some bold color blocking, pick a pair of eye-popping purple shoes. They'll look amazing clashed with the acid yellow of the dress. Choose sleek and simple purple peep-toes; these needn't cost a fortune and should be seen as a low-cost fashion purchase. Remember, this outfit should be fun, vivacious, and not taken too seriously.

I'm not giving you permission to look like a clown, but a lipstick with a purple hue can really help bring this outfit together. It's important not to go too purple or you'll look like a fashion victim. With such bold colored lips, keep your eye makeup simple.

zipper belt

Get your craft head on and take a trip to your local fabric shop. Versace often uses zippers ornamentally, so buy a purple longer-length zipper and turn it into a head-turning belt by sewing on a hook and eye and linking them at the back.

A purple bag could be a step too far in color-themed style, but a rhinestone or crystal bag will look fabulous and is a wardrobe staple that will last a lifetime. These bags tend to be a bit on the pricey side, but can be pressed into service for any evening event.

purple lipstick

crystal bag

A glamorous maxi dress looks amazing whatever your age or figure shape, and when the fabulous length is combined with a halter neckline, you're on to a winner. A halter is great at accentuating your cleavage and keeps attention up top, so it's great if you're wider in the hips than you'd like to be. Make sure the lines aren't cut too low, or your look will go from classy to brassy.

Maxi

BRIGHT

The cut of the dress is paramount, and the empire line is a very flattering option. A gathering of fabric at the front of the dress makes this type of empire line an even more slimming option. The dress already does the hard work and nips you in where it should, so take full advantage of it and add a rhinestone longline necklace. This will elongate your figure even further by drawing the eye down the body and toward your nipped-in waist.

Since the dress shape is so chic, sexy, and slimming, stay away from black and go really Versace with a bold turquoise, a color that is really very wearable and goes with most skin tones. To glam things up even further, add rhinestone shoes and bag for a luxury feel and for true red carpet glamour.

CHANGE THE LOOK

Can you really wear an evening gown to a beach party? Of course you can! Start by eliminating all traces of rhinestones. Place a braided leather belt around your middle and pile on wooden and brass bangles. Use a boho-style scarf as a pashmina and change those crystal strappies for some gladiator sandals.

"Go really
Versace
with a bold
turquoise"

"Silver, nude, and gray work beautifully together"

Take Versace glamour into fall/winter and team a fabulous cocktail dress with key wardrobe basics. A nude-colored cocktail dress, made in a slinky ruched fabric, has Donatella written all over it. Make sure it's fitted and body-hugging around your torso and waist, and a tiny bit of cleavage won't go amiss either.

Bold SILHOUETTE

necklace

The same rules apply to your neck as to your wrist. Statement necklaces can make or break an outfit, but keep them size-appropriate. Faceted crystal stones in a medium size look amazing, simple, and chic.

Keep the length well above the knee for a supersexy edge, but don't worry about showing too much flesh—a pair of charcoal-gray tights will cover you up nicely. The tights mean that this look can be worn by most sizes, but unfortunately it does have an age limit; over 40s should pass this one by.

If you are on the petite side, then the proportions are key, so make sure the dress fits perfectly. Do this with the help of a nifty seamstress, or look in petite sections over the festive period and stock up for the year.

Contrast the fitted quality of the dress with a great wardrobe piece, a sequin tux jacket. Roll up the jacket sleeves or buy one with three-quarter-length sleeves, add a pair of high-heeled silver pumps, and the silhouette created is pure catwalk glamour.

chunky bracelet

matching bag

A gathering of crystal bracelets is perfect for this look, and with your sleeves rolled up all eyes will be on your bling, so keep it bright, shiny, and mega-bold, but don't go too big with the stones or the proportions will look odd.

A nude bag looks fabulous with a matching nude dress and really helps pull the elements of the look together. An oversized bag is not out of the question for petite ladies as long as it's slimline and envelope style.

Having a baby is an amazing experience, but like anything in life it comes with its more challenging aspects. Just because you're pregnant doesn't mean that style needs to go out the window, even if some maternity ranges seem to insist on it. When I've dressed friends or clients who are pregnant, most are adamant that they don't want to spend a fortune, still want to follow the trends, and most of all, despite the morning sickness and an aching back, want to feel fabulous.

PREGNANCY STYLE

SMOCK TOPS

Keep your eyes peeled for empire line or smock dresses and tops in nonmaternity collections. Depending on the season, these can be in abundance and can be worn both casually and formally. The waistline sits under your bust and above your belly, so the fabric below the waistband will comfortably cover your bump, and you can still wear the top postpregnancy.

AUCTION WEBSITES

Always check on an auction website for pregnancy clothes—there are some incredible bargains to be had. But don't feel guilty about making a pricey maternity purchase: unless you're planning another baby, just log on and start selling when you're back to your usual size.

THE LBD

A maternity LBD is an absolute must-have, whether it's from a maternity range or is a good-quality jersey wrap dress from an ordinary store. Dress it up or down, wear it with a denim jacket, a rhinestone necklace, or the latest accessory.

SHOES

Even when you're eight months in, some meetings or events will call for a pair of heels. Get some slim-line flats for your handbag so that style AND comfort are always within easy reach.

COATS

Whether it's summer or winter, buy a swing coat with three-quarter-length sleeves. The shape of the coat will work with your bump and the sleeves have a timeless elegance. A wool version with long, colored gloves will keep you warm and looking fabulous in winter, and a linen version over a T-shirt looks equally chic in summer.

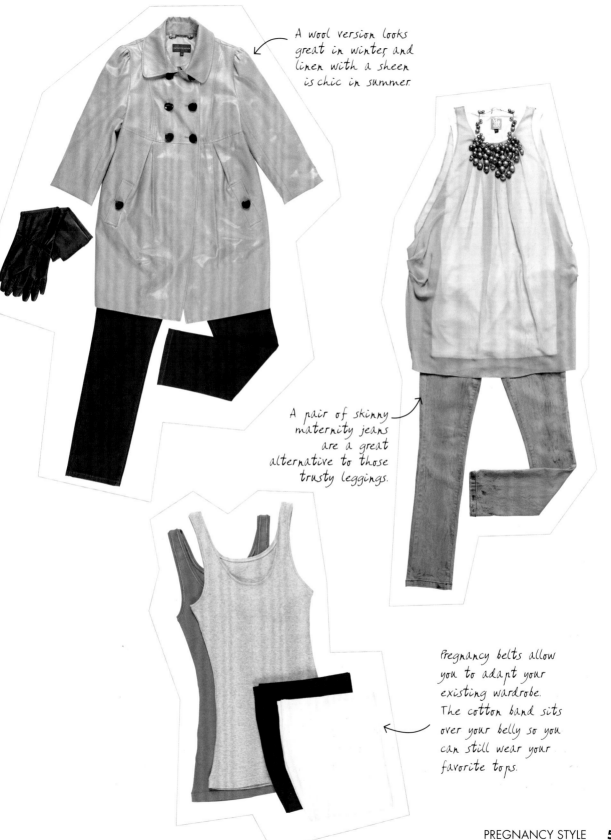

A wool version looks great in winter, and linen with a sheen is chic in summer.

A pair of skinny maternity jeans are a great alternative to those trusty leggings.

Pregnancy belts allow you to adapt your existing wardrobe. The cotton band sits over your belly so you can still wear your favorite tops.

Yves Saint Laurent

MASCULINE TAILORING

In 1971 Bianca stepped out in style to marry Mick Jagger: she was wearing an Yves Saint Laurent cream suit with, apparently, nothing underneath. Since then, Masculine Tailoring, with a twist, has been on every fashionista's style radar.

Get the look

It's the perfect look if you want to be extremely stylish and overwhelmingly elegant at the same time. It's the type of outfit that says, "I'm not interested in trends, just beautiful, classic, lifetime pieces that suit my body shape." The great thing about Masculine Tailoring looks is that they can be taken apart and the individual pieces worn as separates. But when put together, they look perfect in any classy environment, whether it's the Oscars or a family wedding.

Although many designers have played with androgyny, it's YSL that took it to a level where it was utterly wearable. Despite its strong sense of masculinity, these are some of the most feminine pieces you'll ever see, and Mr. Saint Laurent is still considered a pioneer of modern-day fashion. Since his death in 2008, his influences have remained strong for YSL's creative director, Stefano Pilati, who still reworks those signature pieces that made the brand what it is today.

The look may be understated, but it speaks volumes in the style stakes and remains a firm favorite with fashion glitterati and celebrites alike.

Elegant cigarette pants.

NAOMI CAMPBELL
The silhouette this divine suit creates is timeless elegance personified. Although an average black pantsuit may be dull, drab, and masculine to say the least, the cut of these 7/8 cigarette pants oozes sex appeal, while the long, one-button jacket gives a hint of a waist and simply flaunts femininity.

JESSICA BIEL
This is a brave choice by Jessica, and is possibly one of the more masculine-looking suits YSL has sent down the runway. However, the one-button coat accentuates the waist, while those wide-leg, floor-skimming pants lengthen her body and legs to supermodel proportions.

A statement-making dress.

One-button jacket highlights the waist.

A wide leg is so lengthening.

JULIANNE MOORE
This fashion-forward jacket/dress is cute, quirky, and sexy in one. The combination of monochrome tailoring, cleavage, and leg silhouette makes for a headline-grabbing outfit. Take note: with such a statement-making dress, keep accessories to a minimum—a simple black clutch and heels will do the trick. Let the tailoring do the talking!

Here is a version of the iconic outfit Yves Saint Laurent designed, which catapulted the label to the forefront of fashion. The smoking suit with the cigarette-leg pant can be worn by young or old, large or small, and is one of the most versatile combos you'll ever own. Remember, each piece can be worn individually and still make a statement.

Classic TAILORING

We would all love to own an original YSL suit, but with such a hefty price tag that may well never happen. Thankfully, cigarette-leg suits are in abundance season after season in far less pricey shops. The only problem is that the cut of your suit needs to be exquisite, so it's imperative that you take it to a local tailor for final fitting. Make sure you try the suit on in front of your tailor and let him or her start pinning. The difference will be unbelievable, and it will look like you've added an extra zero to that price tag.

Make sure the jacket is one-button, and if it has satin lapels, so much the better. A simple man's tuxedo shirt worn underneath is an original option that's inexpensive but really effective.

statement necklace

A statement necklace adds interest and a girly twist to give your masculine chic a feminine edge. Keep with the monochrome theme and only go for jet-black, larger-than-life stones. Make sure they have angular edges and sit elegantly next to the collarbone.

sequined bag

You can't go overboard on the femininity here, but a black sequined clutch is just the right amount of ladylike glamour. Don't worry about its size or shape—as long as it's sequined and black it will do the job perfectly.

Carrying the monochrome theme through to your footwear is the height of elegance and really balances out the outfit. The platform sole not only makes for more comfort but also seriously adds to the fashion drama.

monochrome heels

"A man's tuxedo shirt worn underneath is an original option"

A cream or ivory suit may not, at first glance, seem to be the most flattering of outfits. However, the savior that is Masculine Tailoring combats the problem of the lighter color. The longer-line jacket is a great slimming aid, because it ends just below your derriere, minimizing a more voluptuous bottom and giving you that all-important extra inch of confidence.

Pale TAILORING

The line the one-button jacket creates draws the eye in at the middle to emphasize, or even create, a waist. The vest acts in a similar way to a corset, cinching and smoothing your waistline.

When this is teamed with a matching pair of every girl's must-have wide-leg pants, you're on track for a great look. When purchasing a pair of pale-colored wide-leg pants, it's worth spending a little bit more and making sure they are lined. With the pants this light in color, it's imperative that you don't see dimply skin, hold-in panty bulges or the dreaded VPL (visible panty line).

One of the biggest benefits of this flattering outfit is its versatility: it can take you to an evening affair, a summer wedding, or even an A-list bash.

black sequined scarf

A sequined evening scarf is a great alternative to jewelry and brings some subtle glimmer to this timeless outfit. Wear the scarf hanging loose—the two lines that run vertically down the front of the body are visually very slimming.

Yves Saint Laurent has become renowned for its cocktail rings. They're not ridiculously pricey, so you may want to splash out, though if you want to keep the expense down, there are similar versions out there.

bold cocktail ring

stiletto shoes

Although there's black in this outfit, under no circumstances should you wear black shoes with a cream suit. It puts the outfit off balance and manages to entirely cheapen the look. A cream stiletto shoe will look fabulous.

"It can take
you to an
evening affair
or summer
wedding"

"Spend a bit more on well-made, well-fitted pants"

Separates are a great tool for curvaceous ladies, and when styled to perfection they can help you look instantly slimmer. Despite what you might think, don't write off the idea of a pair of black skinny pants. They are a wardrobe essential that can easily be dressed up or down.

Tailored
SEPARATES

The ideal length will sit comfortably on your ankle; shin-length styles are a seriously unflattering fashion faux pas, and being too long will ruin the proportions of these figure-fixing beauties. My advice is, don't be scared to spend a bit more on well-made, well-fitted pants —they'll last a lifetime.

With fashion's favorite black down below, it's time to introduce the monochrome look with a bright white fitted shirt. This draws attention to the top of your body and keeps your bottom half as slim as can be. For that ultra YSL style, look for a shirt with a large collar and cuffs. It can be worthwhile going to a specialized shirt store that you might usually associate with men for this. You'll tend to find that the women's shirts they stock fit like a glove and are much more reasonably priced than their designer counterparts.

An open bow tie is a superchic and elegant way to inject the Masculine Tailoring trend into any wardrobe. Wear it as you would usually wear a statement necklace, but allow the lines to run down your body to visually reduce problem cleavage.

cummerbund

A cummerbund is the perfect alternative to a waist belt. It does exactly the same job by pulling you in at the middle and hiding a rogue spare tire. Adjustable cummerbunds are readily available in menswear shops and aren't pricey.

Yves Saint Laurent is famed for its unique and unusual hard-cased evening bags. If you can't get the real deal, there are plenty available in nondesigner shops, or you could explore some vintage stores. Just stick to metallic colorways.

bow tie

hard-cased bag

This is probably the most feminine of all the Masculine Tailoring looks, but without question it has that YSL quality that exudes wealth and glamour. Let's begin with the tailoring: a nipped-in blazer that can be bought in any department store is a really worthwhile investment and an essential part of any capsule wardrobe.

Feminine TAILORING

scarf

ruffle skirt

You need to go for it here: tie a large pussycat bow and make no apologies for it. This is a signature style for YSL and is an easy way to luxe up any look—stiffen your own scarf with spray starch for that expensive boutique feel.

bow bag

The horizontal stripe effect on this skirt is so YSL, but also so unflattering if you're on the larger side. Such a skirt probably shouldn't be worn if you're over a size 12. Choosing black would make it slightly more flattering, but still be cautious.

A bow motif features in many of Yves Saint Laurent's runway accessories and clothing items. Choose a bow-detail bag in black or gray as a simple yet effective way of setting the seal on your couture-esque outfit.

Wear it to work, or with jeans, or even with your favorite frock. Here, it's adding structure and a masculine edge to an otherwise ladylike look. The subtle combination of soft gray fabrics and stark black gives this outfit a real Paris catwalk vibe.

The satin shirt underneath the jacket needs to be lightweight and really quite figure-hugging; anything too loose or bulky will spoil the lines of this sleek runway look. The sophisticated ruffle miniskirt makes this outfit even more chic, and the soft chiffon layers keep it stylish at all times.

As mentioned in the Capsule Wardrobe section (see page 26), a pair of black pumps is a fashion staple. A four-inch heel in patent leather isn't ridiculously high, and the shiny leather tends to last a bit longer than the matte alternative. Remember, shoe repairers can add another season's life to any decent shoe with a spanking new sole. So don't write off past purchases—just care and repair.

"The ruffle miniskirt makes this outfit even more chic"

Yves Saint Laurent was known for its double-breasted men's tuxedos in the 80s and they've adapted these into some fabulous dress styles. Every now and then you may find that some clever store has done a gorgeous look-alike version, but I can assure you these tend to be few and far between and never stay on the shelves for long.

Tailored TUXEDO

So it's time to get creative again and start rummaging around the vintage stores. They are hardly at the top of the style list for men right now, so there's a huge variety of men's double-breasted tuxedo jackets in many vintage stores. This is great news for you, and who knows, you may even find a YSL tux lurking on a rail for next to nothing. You'll then need to take the jacket to your tailor and have the shoulders taken in and the sleeves shortened.

Thankfully, if you're on the petite side an oversized man's jacket will actually be minidress length on you. Just in case it's not, though, keep your modesty intact with thick black tights, a black miniskirt, and a simple lace tank top under the tux. The entire outfit is black, so the jacket and skirt length don't look too extreme.

A black satin envelope clutch can dress up any outfit by giving it some serious after-hours glamour. Now, I know you can barely fit anything in it, but what does that matter when you look so good? Stick to black on black and you can't go too wrong.

CHANGE THE LOOK

This jacket/dress is just too good not to wear as often as possible, so here's a workwear option for you to try. Pop some color behind the jacket and wear it as a coat. Replace the black satin clutch with a structured bag and the booties with a simple pump.

"High-heeled booties add a high-fashion edge"

Giving birth may be the most natural thing in the world, but it is a huge change for your body. You need to give yourself a few weeks in clothes with plenty of give while everything moves back into place and you get used to the gorgeous new bundle of joy in your life.

POST-PREGNANCY FASHION

STRETCH FABRICS

Tops and pants with plenty of Lycra® work well at this stage, because most women shrink fairly rapidly. Don't just go for gray or black—a bit of color will lift your mood and light up your face for all those new baby photos.

TOPS

The smock tops that became such good friends during your pregnancy do need some alterations, but don't worry, it's nothing drastic. A simple belt will change the style enough to stop you from looking like you're still at the four-and-a-half-month stage.

UNDERWEAR

The right underwear is essential and will help you regain confidence in your body. However, a hard-core, all-in-one hold-in might be every girl's best friend, but it's not the best idea when you're trying to breastfeed. Just get some light support panties or some control hose for when you go out.

FIGURE FIXERS

Choose a tailored jacket in a neutral color. This is an instant fashion fix for giving you back a waist and it can be worn with anything: it looks great with denims or even with a tunic and leggings.

It may not be first thing on your list, but a dress with structure will visually melt away the pounds and help flatten that tummy. Look for one in a thicker fabric as it helps hold in even a hint of a jelly belly.

JEANS

A pair of jeans will help you get out of day-to-day leggings hell. You will have to buy them in your "new" size, but don't let that get you down. You don't need to spend a fortune—a cheap pair will do the trick and make you feel a bit more svelte.

Tailoring is a godsend. A one-button boyfriend blazer will work perfectly.

The wrap dress is a wardrobe staple that will never go out of style and is superflattering.

Even pregnancy tunic dresses and tops can get a new lease on life with a wide belt.

Matthew Williamson

GLOBAL BOHO

Global Boho uses a mixture of different ethnic trends from around the world to create a unique blend of textures, styles, and detailing. Obviously it needs a manager to make it chic, wearable, and utterly desirable. Matthew Williamson is the king of all things boho and a fabulous designer of this eclectic style.

Get the look

Matthew launched his label in 1996 after training with eccentric fashion guru Zandra Rhodes, who obviously encouraged his love of the bright and beautiful. He loves ethnic embroidery, and it is a skill he's actually mastered on his travels around the globe. An important part of the Williamson concept is luxury, and all his designs have a lust-worthy Ibiza feel: not the tacky side of Ibiza with the garish nightclubs, the fabulous side with all the yachts! This luxurious element is brought to fruition with his use of metallics, fabulous silks, and his divine cuts.

He also takes inspiration from nature. Key symbols include pretty, oversized peacock feathers, floral designs, and beautiful butterfly prints. The color palette includes signature hot pinks and vivid turquoises as well as the pastels that are so flattering to so many skin tones.

With the proliferation of designer look-alikes in the chain stores, all of these elements can be sourced without having to spend big bucks and then brought together to create your very own take on Global Boho style.

Ethnic embroidery.

MISCHA BARTON
The tunic dress silhouette is a consistent feature in every Matthew Williamson collection. That means they'll always be on trend, and they are just so flattering. The best thing about a tunic is that it covers arms, covers butts, and only exposes legs, which can easily be made the most of with hosiery. All this, and tunics still manage to be supersexy, as Mischa positively proves.

CAT DEELEY

A floor-length maxi is as gracious and gorgeous as can be. The subtle floral pattern and watercolor effect add to the naturally whimsical quality of this ultra-desirable piece. Cat really works the asymmetric line, and her height helps give this dress some serious drama. She loves fashion, and this dress really loves her.

Oversized peacock feathers.

Fabulous floral silk.

Vivid turquoise and pink.

NICKY HILTON

It's the peacock feather motif that's instantly recognizable as Matthew Williamson, and it's key to re-creating this catwalk look without breaking the bank. The vibrant colors of this tunic are another central element of his classy, bohemian, statement-making style.

MATTHEW WILLIAMSON **79**

The combination of a maxi dress and vest is a fashion marriage made in heaven. The maxi has a fantastic silhouette, and even on its own, the floaty, figure-fixing shape can work wonders. When this silhouette is teamed with a subtle-colored paisley print, the pounds will drop off in an instant. The rule for patterns is that the larger you are, the less bold the print should be.

Boho PRINT

If you are size 12 or above, be cautious about a bold, oversized pattern unless it's the same tone as the dress color. Another key rule for maximum impact with your maxi is its length: it's imperative that in bare feet it hits your ankles, or in other words comes to about 1 in. (2.5 cm) above the floor. Any longer and you're likely to trip, any shorter and you'll look like a tree stump. If you find a dress that's perfect except for the length, take it to

a tailor for either shortening, or even lengthening with a band of ribbon sewn to the hem.

On to the vest: the vertical lines that this creates lengthen your body even further, so it's fabulous if you're conscious of your bosom and tummy. The embellished features on the vest are a key design trend to always look for. If you're having a lazy day, throw your vest over a T-shirt for that instant boho vibe.

bangles

ethnic necklance

At first glance gladiators might not appear to be the most flattering shoes for curvy girls. Actually, they are fine—just don't be tempted by ankle-high styles that make ankles look bigger and legs slightly squat. Gladiators will give your maxi a serious fashion edge.

A well-made ethnic necklace can be worn with any outfit. It looks amazing with a boho outfit, but just as good on a tank top or even an evening dress.

A mixture of dark wood and brass bangles instantly creates the ethnic vibe that is synonymous with Global Boho. Make sure you stack them high and layer different designs for a catwalk feel. Try flea markets for low-priced options.

gladiator sandals

"The vertical lines will lengthen your body"

This distinctive Matthew Williamson-esque dress, which clashes turquoise and pink together, is one of the most eye-catching color combinations you could ever wear. To add extra pizzazz, you need to choose some key embellishments. Matthew is a huge fan of stones, sequins, and rhinestones, all applied with the utmost taste.

Boho
COLOR

This particular dress was embellished already, but if your must-have turquoise (or pink) little number is naked of gems, head straight to your local notions store and get creative. Try either fabric glue, a needle and thread, or even badge-making pins on the back of gems—the latter make it easy to mix and match if you change your mind. Keep it chic and stick to embellishing just the neckline.

A short shift dress is ideal for smaller ladies. The proportions it creates give a fabulous optical illusion of you being taller than you actually are.

When it comes to length, mid-thigh or above works best, so you have to be relatively happy with your legs. Fear not—if the thought of baring all fills you with dread, a pair of opaque tights are perfectly acceptable with this outfit.

bracelet

With a fringed shift and all that embellishment, there's no way this outfit could take either a necklace or larger-than-life earrings. So keep your earrings small and go for some statement-making bangles or bracelets. Keep them the same tones as the dress and be the ultimate glamour-puss.

With a turquoise dress, a pink jeweled bag (not too large—remember that oversize can swamp you) with a silver fastener is perfect. The color combination is incredibly catwalk, and that hint of metallic is a fabulous touch.

I'm a matching-shoe-and-bag kind of boy, and this works fabulously when you're clashing two colors. The shoes should be satin, superhigh, and closed-toe to round off the perfect petite outfit.

pink bag

pink heels

"A short shift
dress is ideal
for smaller
ladies"

"Pattern is key in this take on Global Boho"

Matthew Williamson has allowed the maxi to be worn both casually during the day or superglam for the evening; either way, it's fashionable and flattering. For an evening look you need to make sure your maxi's sexily strapless or an elegant halter. Don't worry if you're self-conscious about your upper arms—a lace or silk bolero will look fabulous. Just make sure it's heavily embellished.

Maxi BOHO

P attern is key in this take on Global Boho, so keep your eyes peeled for a bohemian-inspired floral print dress, or if you find any maxi with butterfly detailing, you're on to a winner: the maxi/butterfly combination is as Matthew Williamson as it gets. Add an original touch with a piece of hand-made jewelry: it's easy, honestly it is. Take one peacock feather and wrap the base of the quill with some brass wire and finally make a loop. Thread it onto a purchased long-length chain and you'll have the most amazing, unique bohemian necklace. To add to this style and keep costs down at the same time, pile on the kind of inexpensive, colorful bangles that you can buy for next to nothing in flea markets.

This is one of the few times you'll wear a maxi with heels, but the hem still has to be floor-skimming. One option for lengthening a maxi is to wear a separate maxi skirt underneath in a matching or contrasting color and make a feature out of it.

CHANGE THE LOOK

This high-glamour look can easily be taken down a few notches to make it perfect for a summer barbecue. Replace the peacock necklace with a set of long beads, replace the clutch with a straw bucket bag, and change the embellished fabric belt for a brown leather version. Then simply throw on a denim jacket over the top.

This is an eclectic mismatch of key items that takes layering to a whole new level and is a perfect look for trans-seasonal periods, such as winter-to-spring and summer-to-fall. When working on your version of this look, don't be shy about experimenting with layer combinations—you might be surprised at what works.

Layered
BOHO

A short-sleeved tunic dress is every girl's best friend and can be worn by itself or, as here, over trusty denims. The great thing about a tunic dress is that it shows off your curves, yet it's ideal for covering the tops of arms and problem derrieres. Go for a tunic with a lining so that the top layer can't cling to your curves or your denims, but just hangs and works its magic.

As if that wasn't enough, a faux-fur vest adds both warmth and a fashion edge. Make sure the fur isn't too bulky, because this can sometimes add extra width to your torso. When you're using this much layering it's imperative that you keep the underlying silhouette sleek and fuss-free. Therefore boot-cut jeans are a definite no-no since the added bulk at the bottom of the outfit will detract from the top. If you haven't taken the plunge on the skinny jean front yet, it's not as scary as it seems; with a tunic dress and a pair of killer heels you'll be turning heads for all the right reasons.

bejeweled cuff

Take embellishment one step further and wow the crowd with a supersize jewel. It may cost more than your average cuff, but jewelry this fabulous is worth the splurge. If you stick to a neutral metallic you can dress up any outfit in an instant, and it'll last you a lifetime.

beaded neckline

Fine beadwork and Matthew Williamson go hand in hand, and the color combination of fluorescent pink, white, orange, and purple is a fashion match made in heaven. Look for either paisley pattern swirls or organic shapes such as leaves, butterflies, or flowers.

heels

With so much going on at the top, heels are an essential part of this outfit. They elongate your entire shape and keep things looking sexy. Make sure they are high and work with colors of the outfit for top-to-toe fashionista style.

"A tunic is great for covering problem derrieres"

An embellished silk caftan is one of the greatest buys a woman can make. It's perfect for the beach over your swimsuit, and with wide-leg linen pants or jeans. The idea of a pair of white jeans may usually have you quivering in a corner, but as long as they're boot-cut to balance those curves, they'll be perfect. A chiffon caftan is a great trick for hiding your bottom and disguising chunky thighs.

Beach
BOHO

woven belt

Most of these caftans will usually be found in the swimwear department, but don't let this fool you —they're essential as part of any Global Boho wardrobe or in any vacation suitcase. Don't be scared of bold prints—the translucency of the fabric softens the overall look, keeping it feminine, fashionable, and flattering.

Everything's done for you here with all the embellishment around the neckline and middle of this caftan. The nipped-in middle naturally pulls you in at your narrowest part and although the rest is loose-fitting, your silhouette can be seen, making this a very sexy look. Don't forget a basic purple tank top for underneath—you don't want to show too much!

feather earrings

Don't go for anything too over-the-top—you don't want to look like you're playing dress-up. A simple pair of feathered beauties is just right for this easy-to-wear look, and very much in the Matthew Williamson style.

Enhance your waist further with a woven belt. It's a great tool for taking the look from day to night and adding extra wow to your outfit. In keeping with the boho theme, try matching the color in the belt with your caftan. If you can't, try a neutral colorway for a tip-top look.

These embellished sandals are your perfect partner at home or abroad; they can be packed easily and are worth their weight in gold. The combination of the already statement-making metallic leather and the oversized gems will seriously glamorize any outfit. Thankfully, because they're flat, you have A-list style with comfort.

embellished sandals

"A silk caftan is feminine, flattering, and fashionable"

For many women, buying a swimsuit, or worse still a bikini, is a complete ordeal. But in fact it's no different from any other fashion purchase—you just need to get the right style for your figure.

SWIMWEAR GUIDE

PRINTS
Don't shy away from prints—fun and flirty print bikinis will look fantastic on most sizes. However, as a rule of thumb, the bigger you are, the smaller the pattern should be. And always beware of the dreaded horizontal stripe. If patterns aren't your thing but you still want glamour, go for metallics.

TANKINIS
These long-top bikinis are fantastic for most shapes and sizes, because they hide the dreaded tummy area. Go for one with a high-cut bottom —it'll be magic at lengthening legs—while a halter-neck tankini is perfect for pear shapes— it increases your bust size and slims the hips.

BIKINIS
Halter necks work best on small boobs and make the most of what you've got. Bandeaus, on the other hand, work against them, flattening and squashing your assets. For those with a fuller bust, it's worthwhile getting fitted for a bikini to avoid unexpected exposure in the waves.

If your beach body doesn't fill you with confidence, then beware of side-tying bikinis. Also, steer clear of shorts-style bikini bottoms if you have big hips; a horizontal line across the body will do you no favors!

Try mixing and matching bikini separates if you're different sizes top and bottom.

ACCESSORIES
Use accessories to give any bikini an instant fashion makeover. Bright, statement jewelry is always flattering because it diverts attention away from problem areas. Another trick is to play with proportions; try using an oversized beach bag to make you look smaller. Trust me, it works!

Remember that beachwear is the one place where having everything matching isn't a fashion faux pas, so get the matching caftan and sarong and ease yourself in gradually.

ONE-PIECE SWIMSUITS
One-pieces are still incredibly glam and flattering and are perfect if you're more mature. When it comes to cutout one-pieces, beware; they may be on trend but certainly aren't good for a tan line.

A medium-sized print will work on most figures.

Timeless and ageless.

Great for pear shapes.

Seriously glam.

If you've got it, flaunt it.

Side ties can lengthen legs.

Miu Miu/Prada

CUTE AND QUIRKY

Prada began life in 1913, but only became the quirky design powerhouse we know and adore when Miuccia Prada took over the reins in 1978. Since then it's gone from strength to strength, and she's become one of the most respected leaders of fashion, a modern-day Coco Chanel if you wish.

Get the look

One of Miuccia's most famous design philosophies is making the ugly beautiful. Whether it's wrinkly stockings, grandma-style bags, or even 1960s turbans, she has the Midas touch and has turned a long list of "ugly" items into must-have fashion classics. This theme continued into her other label, Miu Miu. This began in 1992 and is a more youthful line. It allowed people to start having a bit more fun with fashion, whether with big bows, full skirts, crazy heels, or futuristic fabrics.

Miu Miu and Prada lead the way with some of the most innovative clothing and accessories the catwalks have seen in decades. Which takes us to everyone's favorite part, the shoes. Both labels design some of the most to-die-for shoes the fashion pack has ever seen. Whether they feature oversized gems, platform soles, origami detailing, or sculptured heels, they're all fabulous.

Although Miuccia's eccentric designs are constantly changing, there are core shapes, cuts, and styles that are instantly recognizable. A sculptural, shaped skirt is about as Prada as you can get, and oversized coats with mixtures of textures are a close and gorgeous second.

Sculptural shapes.

REESE WITHERSPOON
This dress has fashionista written all over it and takes some courage to pull off with style. The oversize shoulders may look unwearable, but as you can see, Reese looks every bit the style icon. The solid black silhouette keeps it flattering and utterly fabulous.

NATALIE PORTMAN
This beautifully cut, ladylike dress could work on anyone, but it's the sophisticated combination of two different shades of navy and a dash of purple that really sets it apart. A similar effect could be worked with two shades of gray and a flash of contrasting color.

Sophisticated navy and purple combo.

Perfect Peter Pan collar.

Tulip-shaped mini skirt.

CHLOË SEVIGNY
There aren't many celebs out there who could work this high-fashion trend without looking ever-so-slightly like a dolly, but Chloë certainly can. The signature Peter Pan collar and tulip-shaped mini skirt are as fashion-savvy as you can get. Mix this with some cute-as-they-come high ankle boots for optimum quirky Miu Miu style.

This is as Cute and Quirky as it gets. The Miu Miu look is big news in Japan, and this outfit has a definite Harajuku Girl quality; it's for the fashion-forward (and twenty-somethings) only! Remember, this look isn't meant to be taken too seriously and should be worn with confidence and a smile.

Quirky GIRL

Many of the items included in this look could, by themselves, be considered prim, proper, and extremely ladylike. Only when worn together and added to a high-fashion piece, such as a volume skirt, does the ordinary turn into the extraordinary. Equally, any of the accessories in this outfit can be put with the most basic garment for an undeniably Miu Miu edge.

Firstly, a short, puff-sleeve jumper is an essential, just as long as it has that all-important round collar. This is taking granny chic to a whole new level, but make sure you don't go for granny sizes. The better the cut, the better the overall look.

Combine this with a high-waisted volume skirt. The sculptural quality of these skirts can actually be far more flattering that you might imagine as the shape is great at disguising troublesome behinds and heavier hips. You can play it safe with the color if you wish, but for a truly quirky edge choose ruby red, popping purple, or glistening gold.

There's a brutal fashion rule when it comes to hair bands: they may be an incredibly effective way to get the Miu Miu look, but if you're over 35 you can look as though you've raided your daughter's dressing table. For those under 35, gems and bows are the best embellishments.

hair band

bow clutch

For a more age-appropriate way of wearing bows, have them on your bag. An oversized bow bag is a great way of changing even the dullest of outfits into a fashion masterpiece.

shoe boots

Some quirky shoe boots are fabulous for adding a fashionista edge to any outfit. Although the lines working across the ankle may not be the most flattering of looks, you can minimize the fashion faux pas by teaming them with thick black tights.

"Sculpted skirts are great for troublesome behinds"

Prada in particular is known for its simple lines and oversized shapes. At first glance, this duster-style coat worn over a pleated detail skirt may not appear to be the most flattering outfit. However, the oversized tailoring of this coat is very effective at covering lumps and bumps you'd rather not show. The chiffon layer on the skirt also adds to the flattering look.

Quirky DETAILING

The short-sleeve detailing is a key style in Prada outerwear, and don't be scared about layering a long sleeve under the short sleeve. Again, this is a signature Prada look that is so easily achieved. The combination of a smooth metallic satin and the strong silhouette of the black woolen turtleneck gives this outfit a catwalk edge, while still remaining completely wearable. Notice the two vertical lines the coat creates down the body. This gives an amazing optical illusion that can take two dress sizes off you.

Although all the items of clothing are very beautiful, on someone more mature there is the danger of looking dowdy, so add those accessories! A quality leather bag with tortoiseshell details will get the fashion radar bleeping, and you can even fit the kitchen sink in there, too. When this is combined with a superglam statement necklace and knock-'em-dead heels, you'll be at the front of the fashion pack. Although there are some great imitation Miu Miu shoes around, the real deal could be the one fashion investment that you'll never regret.

CHANGE THE LOOK
This high-fashion work look can be worn as weekend style and still have an essence of Prada. Keep the jacket and the bag and change the skirt and turtleneck for a scoop-neck black T-shirt and a boot-cut pair of indigo denims (indigo's very Prada). Get rid of the heels and comfy it up with a pair of bejeweled flats.

"A signature Prada look that can so easily be achieved"

"It highlights a slender midriff, giving a sexy edge"

This is as chic, simple, and minimal as can be, and has the Prada stamp all over it. A knee-length fitted jumper is a versatile piece that every wardrobe deserves. It may not come across as one of the sexiest items, but it can be dressed up or down and worn day or night. A well-tailored dress should show off assets and hide imperfections.

Cute
CHIC

This entire outfit has a utilitarian air about it and the slate-gray of the jumper adds to that feel. Although Prada can sometimes show quite shapeless garments it's important that your jumper is tailored to flaunt that womanly shape (visiting a tailor for fitting adjustments may not be a bad idea).

When it comes to the shirt, cornflower blue is the color of choice. Again, make sure that it's fitted and, most importantly, buttoned right up to the neck. This little detail turns the outfit from workwear into high fashion.

To enhance the shapely feel of your fitted dress and shirt, a very simple black waist belt is an invaluable asset. It highlights your slender midriff, giving the look a sexy edge.

Girls often forget that double-cuff shirts aren't just for the guys. Combine this cuff with simple, elegant cufflinks for a chic, glamorous touch. This isn't just an office-worthy look—a more showstopping cufflink will raise the style stakes in one easy step.

cufflinks

granny bag

This is a prime example of turning the ugly into the beautiful. The black granny-style bag with comedy-sized clasp is both as classic and as fashionable as can be. Try searching for similar bags in vintage shops and bag a bargain.

jeweled shoes

To keep in tune with the rest of the outfit, the shoes are sleek and simple, yet still irresistibly gorgeous. The oversized stones on these satin heels have a definitive Prada and Miu Miu feel to them. They are great at adding an edge of glamour to any minimal outfit.

The gorgeous combination of teal and black is incredibly sophisticated, but has a cute and quirky edge. When the different textures of glass, wool, silk, sequins, and leather are put together, this outfit goes from basic to amazing in a few easy steps. It's the mixture of textures that gives this look its catwalk feel.

Quirky
TEXTURES

black boots

Black boots are a wardrobe staple that no woman could live without. The chunky heel on these are perfect for adding those all-important inches, yet still manage to be comfortable and chic.

necklace collar

If you can thread a needle, then you can do this. Take one statement necklace and loosely tack it onto the front neckline of the dress. A sheath with this amount of detailing could set you back a small fortune, so just do it yourself and then remove it when bored.

tote bag

Oversized bags may be big fashion news, but be very careful if you're on the petite side. Anything oversized—whether they're glasses, bows, or bags—can make it look as though you've shrunk in the wash. Either go for smaller styles, or in this case an average-size patent bag to finish the look.

Obviously the basis of this look is the trusty LBD. It's an item of clothing that can be changed instantaneously, whether it be with a pair of heels, by layering something underneath, or, as here, by adorning it with jewels. If you are a petite lady and have difficulty finding the perfect LBD, then be sure to try the Internet. There are some great petite sites out there, perfect for wardrobe staples, and all usually have a reliable returns policy.

Keeping on the two tone theme, a pair of opaque teal tights covers legs, while the black boots are surprisingly comfortable with their chunky heel and lovable platform sole.

As for the beanie, don't think I'm mad; it's all about that weird and wonderful runway look that only Prada and Miu Miu can do. But do give your beanie a girlie edge by bejeweling it with a statement pin. The way to wear it is high off your forehead and slouchy at the back.

"Add a girlie edge to your beanie with a jeweled brooch"

Prada and Miu Miu's oversized, sculptural shapes can cover a multitude of sins, but when worn incorrectly will give an average-sized woman all the figure attributes of a sack of potatoes. So please approach with caution. The best way forward is to take figure-fixing wardrobe basics and simply Prada them up.

Quirky BASICS

Key trends include flesh tones, embellishment, leather bows, and glitzy shoes. Let's start with those flesh tones and combine them with a longline coat; it's a definite winner. The lines elongate you, it covers your derriere, and is perfect for each and every season. For ultimate flattery, make sure you cinch it in with a good old-fashioned waist belt.

As for the jeans, go for a slim-leg straight cut. This will give you a similar silhouette to wearing a skinny jean but without the unflattering squeeze; instead they will show your wonderful womanly curves and gorgeous behind.

The length of the denims is also very important. It's worth having a specific pair of jeans for flats and another for heels. When in flats, denims should always be ¼ in. (5 mm) off the ground.

sunglasses

Sunglasses with the stylized shape of a butterfly are "oh so Prada" and have a distinctive fashion-editor vibe about them. This obvious shape can be purchased in many less expensive chain stores for a fraction of the price.

Bows are an essential ingredient for a cute and quirky look; just don't be put off by the supersized styles. A black patent bow belt looks fabulous over a coat, but try it over an LBD, or even over a plain white shirt, for a different look.

bow belt

encrusted pumps

Stop the press! The Miu Miu encrusted heel is the hottest shoe around. Although there are some picture-perfect copies out there, the originals won't break the bank and will survive season after season. Go on, treat yourself!

"It covers
your behind
and is perfect
each and
every season"

Can a woman have too many pairs of shoes? I think not. However, you can't afford everything, so here is some advice to help you choose what to put in your closet and what to just lust after in the shop.

SHOE STYLE

PLATFORM SOLES

Platform soles are an absolute godsend for any woman. They allow you the skyscraping height of a serious stiletto, but with some much-needed added comfort. Here's how it works: the extra height given by the platform sole of the shoe is taken off the ridiculous height of the heel. Happy days!

STRAPS

Ankle straps may add security when you're out and about, but they have a horrible habit of turning your lovely ankles into thick, chunky cankles. An ankle strap is perfectly fine as long as it sits at the top of your foot, well below your ankle. Any higher is a definite no-no.

BOOTS

High-top boots for winter are an essential part of any woman's wardrobe and can easily be dressed up or down. Make sure the length finishes just below your knee. Any higher can look a little trashy and any lower can turn you into a hobbit.

WEDGES

Wedges are the answer to every woman's prayers come the summer. They give you the height and the glamour of high heels, but with the stability of a little kitten heel. If you tend to have wobbly ankles and are nervous about wearing heels, try these for size.

PUMPS

Nude-colored pumps are an invaluable addition to any wardrobe. They can be worn with any outfit to any occasion and have serious leg-lengthening capabilities. A pair of black pumps are also a wardrobe staple; look for patent ones rather than matte black leather. The shiny leather is ultra-glamorous and actually very practical and hard-wearing.

MUST-HAVES

Statement shoes can transform a really average outfit into a something very special. They may not be practical items, but there are occasions when you have to let your heart, not your head, do the talking.

Loving the platform sole.

Wear them with any outfit to any occasion.

The perfect mood lifter.

Stable, practical, and gorgeous.

couldn't live without them.

The perfect ankle strap.

Vivienne Westwood

BRITISH ECCENTRIC

From the mid-1970s right up to this very minute, Vivienne Westwood has been, and is still, an icon of British fashion. Her monumental influence has shaped the dress sense of entire generations, and she's still the eccentric grande dame of UK fashion.

Get the look

Fabulously cut dress.

Westwood's fashion origins in the punk movement shaped her belief in individuality and in stepping outside conventions to create unique styles. These two angles had a huge effect on the fashion world, and the plethora of resulting looks range from low-key to hard-core—you choose.

She's a designer who's loved by women of all ages, shapes, and sizes and who can create womanly curves on the skinniest of girls, while making the most of fuller-figured women. The female form inspires her, and her fabulously cut clothes show it off beautifully. They nip in your waist and push up your bosom, creating an unmistakably Westwood silhouette.

Another big inspiration for Westwood is traditional tailoring, and her understanding of pattern cutting allows her to create shapes that might look extraordinary, but are easy and comfortable to wear. Her technical skills and leader-of-fashion designs have seen her named British Designer of the Year three times, and that's a serious accolade.

Dame Vivienne Westwood, DBE (Dame Commander of the British Empire, an honorary title bestowed by the Queen), has a quintessentially British style that, with its combination of tartan, corsetry, pirate, and punk, has made her famous and hugely popular around the globe.

SHARON OSBOURNE

As a more mature lady, Sharon knows what suits her and knows exactly what her womanly assets are. She's a huge fan of Vivienne Westwood, because it cinches in her waist, boosts her bosom and still covers the tops of her arms. In addition, the longer length of this dress has red-carpet glamour written all over it; what more could a woman want?

ERIN O'CONNOR

Supermodel Erin does Vivienne proud by giving this eccentric tartan dress an added British quirky style. The combination of hosiery and lace-up shoes is Westwood through and through. It might not be the easiest look to carry off, but if you're going to do it, be cool, confident, and catwalk-savvy.

Signature check and quirky cut.

cut inspired by the female form.

KIM CATTRALL

Kim's all about sensuality and made a brilliant choice with this rocking red frock. It flaunts her waist, cleavage, and legs, all without looking even the slightest bit tacky. She's living fashion proof that no matter what your age, a Westwood dress is a fail-safe, sexy investment.

If you're up for making an investment, a Red Label Vivienne Westwood suit will last you a lifetime, and surprisingly won't cost a fortune. The shape is sublime and will never go out of fashion. Vivienne knows exactly how to cut for a woman, and a suit like this is the perfect example of working the shape you have.

Tailored ECCENTRIC

Its figure-fixing lines show every inch of your fabulous waist, create a to-die-for cleavage, and make a larger bottom one of your greatest assets. Choose a plain color or a signature tartan weave; either is ultra-flattering and supersexy.

If your bank balance won't stretch to an original Westwood, then occasionally a Vivienne-inspired jacket or suit, such as the one shown here, will crop up in a more affordable store. If you see one of these beauties, buy it immediately! Key features to look out for are a diagonally cut, double-breasted line that draws the eye down your figure, an open neck that gives you the chance to show cleavage, and a pencil skirt that hits you exactly on the knee.

A word of warning: on cheaper versions make sure that the tartan is cut on the diagonal and not the horizontal. Remember that a horizontal line instantly adds visual pounds.

Vivienne's designs are all about taking things to an extreme, and these oversized pearls do exactly that.

CHANGE THE LOOK
This "don't mess with me" work look can be turned into a weekend outfit in a flash. Change the skirt for a pair of skinny gray jeans and the Mary Janes for a pair of beige cutout shoe-boots. Replace the granny bag with a slouchy duffel-style bag, and the top with a deep red T-shirt.

"An ultra-
flattering
and supersexy
look"

This look has British Eccentric written all over it and requires a stylish attitude and the confidence to work it like a true fashionista. Let's begin with the basic silhouette of a cream, fine-knit sweater. Make sure it has a relatively high, round neckline and is fitted to perfection.

Layered ECCENTRIC

Wear a flesh-colored bra with this, because cream fine knits are notoriously bad for showing black or white underwear in different lights. Then get creative with the skirts. A single tartan skirt will look great, but try being a bit daring and layering one skirt on top of another. Make sure both skirts aren't made of thick fabric, which will add too much bulk. The idea is to layer the thinner fabric skirt over the heavier one and pin up the outer layer with a fabulous brooch to reveal the underlayer's contrasting tartan pattern. This instantly gives you the Westwood feel without spending a fortune.

Remember that fashion's not brain surgery, and it needs to be taken with a pinch of salt sometimes. Always experiment, and have a good giggle! Give it a winter twist with a black top and thick tights.

lace collar

You can find these in notions stores, and the manmade fiber versions usually cost next to nothing. Instead of getting the needle and thread out, try wearing this as you would a necklace and use a simple hook and eye to attach it.

Rather than picking out a basic faux gem pin, it's time to head straight to the vintage stores, or even to your granny's jewelry box. Try to keep in line with Vivienne's quirky vibe.

vintage brooch

round-toed shoes

Ribbon details on shoes are so Westwood and demonstrate real fashion snazziness. When you go for a more fashion-forward shoe, try wearing it in a neutral colorway to get as much use as possible.

"Get creative with skirts— try being a bit daring"

"Nipping in your waist and boosting your bosom"

A pussycat-bow blouse may not be on any curvier girl's fashion wish list. Its sculptural quality is overpowering, adds bulk to your chest, and doesn't exactly pull you in at the waist. But you're forgetting the magic of tailoring, which allows you to wear trends that would otherwise be completely inappropriate.

Shapely ECCENTRIC

As you can see, the tailored vest does all the hard work here. Its shape is very Westwood, nipping in your waist and boosting your bosom. If the vest you find isn't a perfect fit, then a trip to an alterations shop will give it a luxe vibe. When it comes to the pants, make sure they're either wide-leg or straight cut. Both styles will elongate and slim your shape and give the outfit that vampy edge.

As you can see, this outfit is pinstriped, and that's not by chance. A pinstripe is one of fashion's best optical illusions. It visually melts away the pounds by lengthening your entire figure, and it doesn't have to be relegated to an office environment. Try mixing and matching pinstripe pieces with more casual items such as denims and T-shirts or a crisp white shirt and statement necklace for another stylish dimension.

I'm not big on label flaunting and find it rather déclassé, but there are two exceptions. The first is Chanel's double C's and the second is Vivienne Westwood's classic orb. It's instantly recognizable, and an orb pin is a speedy way of designering-up a more affordable outfit.

It's imperative that you add a supersexy element to this outfit. The tailoring may add to those sexy curves, but the lack of flesh requires an injection of height. A sassy pair of skyscraping heels will look amazing. These beauties will become a wardrobe staple.

pearl bracelets

orb pin

Oversize jewelry looks amazing on curvier girls—it's a great trick for balancing out larger hips and behinds. Try wearing a larger-than-life pearl bracelet to add an extra catwalk element, and then multiply it by two—but always on the same arm.

Westwood heel

Vivienne was an inventor of punk and brought pirate fashion into the mainstream, so a nod to both trends is essential for a true British Eccentric look. A pirate-style jacket can easily be found in lighter tones during the spring/summer seasons, or in darker shades during fall/winter seasons. Look for nautical details, and a brocade finish is a great added extra

Pirate ECCENTRIC

For a pirate jacket to look really authentic it must have at least six buttons. The shorter length of this garment really suits a more petite frame and is one of those amazing "fling it on" pieces that can make even the most simple of outfits catwalk-worthy. Be sure the length hits the middle of your derriere and no lower, or the proportions of the outfit will be ruined. Team the jacket with a simple, long-length striped T-shirt. The difference in lengths causes an optical illusion and actually elongates your figure massively, plus it covers your bottom, too.

To round off your look, a pair of pale skinny jeans will show off a perfectly silhouetted figure.

doily stencils

lace shoes

black & white lace pins

Have some creative fun and layer doilies on top of a T-shirt. Then spray a fine mist of black paint, allowing some areas to become darker than others. Remove the doilies and allow to dry. Voilà! Your very own hand-painted T-shirt!

A nude-colored shoe with a black lace overlay adds a sexy edge to even the plainest of outfits and is a great tool for tying in lace detailing elsewhere in an outfit. It works perfectly with your homemade pins, and the height of the heel seals the deal for perfect petite proportions.

Go down to your local craft store and buy a button- or badge-making kit. Next, take a quick trip to a notions store to buy swatches of lace trimmings in black and white. Place black lace over white paper and then seal them in the badge-making press. Do the same with white lace on black paper in every size possible.

"It's perfectly punk with a fabulous feminine edge"

"Minimize problem thighs, hips, or tummies"

A Vivienne Westwood shirt is a designer purchase that'll stand you in good stead for years to come. The price tends to be incredibly reasonable for its quality and cut, and it'll add an air of fashionista quirkiness to any basic outfit. Wear it formally with pants or more casually with denims.

Statement ECCENTRIC

pin

Keep with the monochrome trend and get your mitts on a vintage-inspired lace pin. Imitation antique pins can be readily picked up for a fraction of the cost of the real thing and will work wonderfully with this quirky look. Size really does matter here: go big and bold.

oversized bracelet

black patent pump

The shirt is nipped in at the waist and therefore minimizes your midriff area. This is helped along by some attention-grabbing oversized details. The collar tends to be bigger than on an average shirt and is a figure-fixing wonder. Its larger-than-life nature draws all attention up and away and makes bigger areas of your body appear smaller. This is echoed in the oversized sleeves, which are another fabulous tool for minimizing problem tummies, hips, or thighs.

Since the shirt is making such a statement, less is more when it comes to the rest of the outfit. Keep it simple with a black, soft leather waist belt to slim that silhouette even further.

A pair of flat-fronted, side-fastening wide-leg gray pants are incredibly sleek, and you should know by now how flattering any wide-leg trouser can be. Just make sure that when wearing the side-fastening kind you wear some seriously supportive underwear.

A single bracelet in the same style as the pin will look amazing. On the other hand, a collection of smaller, beaded bracelets will look also incredible. They don't need to match in size and shape, just keep them all pearl or black and pile them high.

One signature shape in Westwood shoes is a slightly rounded toe. You can still get the Westwood feel with a pump; just make sure that the pointed toe isn't too sharp, and always look for a platform sole (another one of Vivienne's key details).

Whether it's a trip to the sales or a trawl through the vintage shops, bargain-hunting is serious business, and you need to prepare properly, or you may kick yourself later.

BAG YOURSELF A BARGAIN

SALES

When you go shopping at sales, take a bottle of water; a hard-core sale is hot and exhausting. Dehydration can make you tired, and then you'll lack that all-important sales concentration.

Dress properly for sales shopping: this is important. Wear flats when you're hitting the sidewalk but take a pair of high-heeled shoes in your bag; these are invaluable when trying on bargain finds. Wear layers, including a simple tank top and a pair of leggings, for changing on the shop floor. That way you can try on with no lines and keep your decency intact. Also, do wear a multiway bra so you can view any dress or top to its best effect.

Keep repeating your sale mantra: "Will I wear it, do I need it, and why didn't I buy it when it was full price?" If you can answer these three points positively, then bag yourself a bargain.

Try not to buy on the first day of a sale. Stores always lower their prices pretty quickly, and you could save yourself an extra 30 percent. However, do go early in the day to beat the crowds. Ask about return policies just in case you change your mind. Many stores change their policy as soon as reductions happen.

Lastly, leave your man at home. It will just end in divorce!

VINTAGE SHOPS

Always try things on in thrift and vintage shops—remember that there are no returns. In a vintage shop or yard sale feel free to haggle, but it's a social faux pas to haggle in a thrift shop.

Head for well-to-do neighbourhoods to find those must-have designer buys. The wealthier the local inhabitants, the better things they give to their thrift shops.

Don't be scared to buy things that might not fit perfectly—a tailor costs very little and can work wonders to make outfits fit like a glove.

Be careful when buying on auction websites—always stick to trusted sellers and read the feedback. If you do have any queries, don't be afraid to email the seller any questions or ask for additional pictures.

Whether it's thrift, vintage, or website, be prepared to spend some time and rummage. Those hidden treasures are not usually staring you in the face.

Make sure delicate pieces are in good condition or at least repairable.

A vintage coat with skinny jeans is so fashion pack!

A vintage accessory can make an outfit.

Don't just look for designer items; mainstream labels can be found in abundance.

Giorgio Armani

ITALIAN CHIC

You won't find any vibrant colors, extraordinary shapes, or outré fashion here. The phrase, "less is more" could have been invented by Giorgio Armani to describe his pared-down, perfectly balanced outfits with simple lines, elegant silhouettes, and tremendously flattering cuts.

Get the look

His clothes are beloved by the inhabitants of Hollywood, to the extent that the Oscar red carpet can sometimes seem to be an Armani fashion show. His tailoring for men has always been outstanding, and the way in which he's adapted that for women is a joy. Simple, elegant, yet with a serious undertone of sexiness, that's what sums up each and every collection Mr. Armani sends down the runways.

Soft tonal hues are synonymous with Armani: mix taupe with cream, slate gray with silver, and soft navy with black to get this look. All the color choices are about subtlety and letting the sublime cut and style of each garment to do the talking.

One of the signatures of Armani is the use of beautiful textures, but his true genius is in the way he clashes them together. Think sequins with raw silk and thick satin with starched linen. When combined with the subtle palette he loves so much, these textures create a luxury feel that sums up true Italian chic.

With the combination of such beautiful colors and simple, flattering cuts, the overall essence of the Armani brand is luxury at its finest. Thankfully the key colors, textures, and shapes can be purchased at small cost, and when correctly worn together you can get a luxury look without the luxury price tag.

Sleek silhouette.

CATE BLANCHETT
This sleek suit silhouette is as Armani as it gets. The neutral metallic colorway and simple lines make it an all-time fashion masterpiece. The strong shoulders are a signature Armani detail and add a sophisticated edginess, while the tapered pants keep it feminine and ultra-elegant.

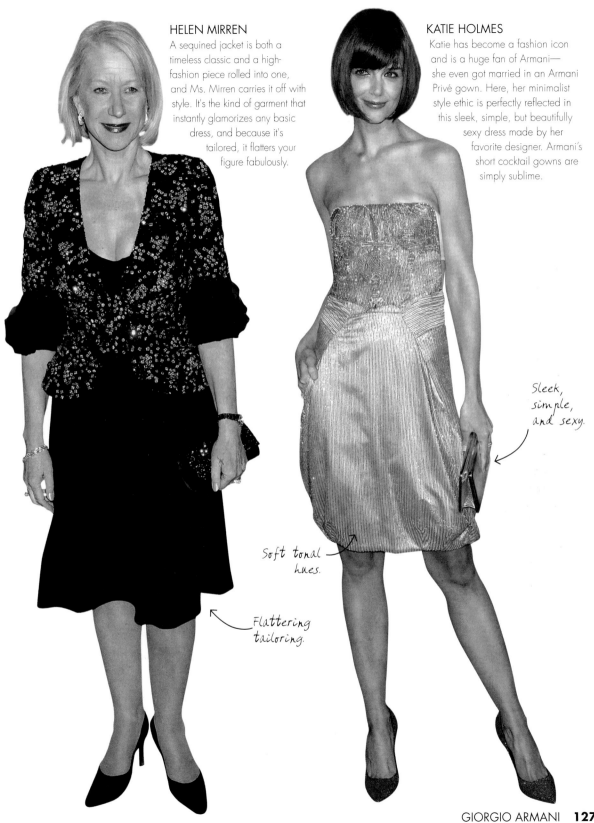

HELEN MIRREN

A sequined jacket is both a timeless classic and a high-fashion piece rolled into one, and Ms. Mirren carries it off with style. It's the kind of garment that instantly glamorizes any basic dress, and because it's tailored, it flatters your figure fabulously.

KATIE HOLMES

Katie has become a fashion icon and is a huge fan of Armani—she even got married in an Armani Privé gown. Here, her minimalist style ethic is perfectly reflected in this sleek, simple, but beautifully sexy dress made by her favorite designer. Armani's short cocktail gowns are simply sublime.

Sleek, simple, and sexy.

Soft tonal hues.

Flattering tailoring.

A perfectly coordinated, elegant skirt and jacket combo—not a suit—is the epitome of style and sophistication. With its sculptural qualities and subtle mixture of colors, plus the ideal accessories, it gives an incredibly wealthy look. As you can see, it isn't an aging style either. The nipped-in separates cling in all the right places, making this outfit anything but frumpy.

Chic SEPARATES

Although Armani is known for simple yet effective color combinations of grays, taupes, and beiges, the one and only pattern that crops up on every runway show is a small check. This follows through the Emporio, the Giorgio, and even the homeware ranges. In other words, whether it's wide-leg pants, a pencil skirt, or a tailored jacket, when you see the right checks, make sure you buy them. Sculpted

skirts can be found in lots of clothing ranges, and many pay a respectful homage to Mr. Armani (I'm sure he's delighted!). Again, when you find one that's a good shape for you, hand over the cash immediately. The skirt needs to nip you in at the waist and hit you at the knee. The fan detail on this skirt elongates the figure, but if you have larger thighs then look for a tulip-style skirt—it'll hide them beautifully.

statement necklace

When Armani does jewelry it's done with style, and a key statement necklace is the only way forward for an absolutely killer minimal look.

fan-shaped bag

This may not be the easiest item to find, but when you do, don't let it pass you by—the fan motif is signature Armani. So although you may not be able to fit anything in it, this bag will give an Armani twist to the simplest of looks.

The all-important waist belt adds that youthful edge to this otherwise classic outfit. It also gives a focal point to the jacket and creates a fabulous waist, even if you don't have one. Try using a darker color for the belt to visually reduce that waist size even further.

waist belt

"The fan detail on the skirt elongates your figure"

"If youth is on your side, go for harem pants"

Whether you style it with a pair of jeans and a simple tank top or with a basic cocktail dress, a tailored sequined jacket adds a glamorous and fashionable edge to even the plainest of outfits. Don't forget, it's also a great tool for covering the upper arms while keeping maximum sparkle—you don't have to resort to a frumpy pashmina or a shrug.

Sequin

CHIC

One particular element of Armani's classic look is the playfulness of proportions. In this version of Italian Chic, the longline jacket and the high-waist harem pants work beautifully together and are ultra-flattering.

A pair of raw silk pants are a real wardrobe must-have; they're extremely elegant but also supercomfy—a rare combination. Depending on your age, either go for wide-legs or harem pants, which give your look an up-to-the-minute catwalk edge. Thin satin and silk pants are notorious for picking up static and clinging to your legs, so always carry a folded-up dryer sheet in your bag: when brushed across the fabric it instantly reduces static for that oh-so-desirable silky-smooth line.

For a homemade Armani-style statement necklace, take one medium-sized tassel attached to thin rope and just pop it over your head. Why not add one to your bag to double the chicness?

CHANGE THE LOOK
Rock up your Armani palette and stride out in style. The combination of an unstructured sequined jacket, stone-washed denims, and black tank top is incredibly striking. Stick with the tassel necklace but change the bag for a metallic number. Add to the look by going for some matching metallic flats.

The combination of taupe and cream is simple and it oozes Italian Chic. Mix in some pewter highlights and darker taupe tone to create drama and depth. When this is matched with the ruffle detailing that can be seen time and time again in so many Giorgio Armani runway shows, it creates a timeless classic and showstopping look.

Ruffled
CHIC

No Armani-esque daytime dress is ever above the knee—it's those womanly curves that create the sexiness, not any exposed flesh. The ruffles running down the center of this particular frock are a godsend for disguising troublesome tummies. The key is to always look for ruffles that work vertically down the body and not horizontally, as those can pile on the pounds.

Another great trick for decreasing lumps and bumps is a pair of hold-in support tights. There are lots of different brands available, and these tights mean no VPL whatsoever, creating a svelte contour and filling you with confidence.

Team this dress with a close-fitting fine-knit cardigan in complementary cream and belt it in to minimize the waist and maximize those curves. Make sure the cardigan finishes below the waist; a shorter length will spoil the perfect proportions of this gorgeous, classic Italian outfit—timeless, ageless, and utterly desirable.

A cheap and effective way to elongate your figure and cinch in that waist is a homemade rope belt. This kind of rope, and the small tassels, can be found either in haberdashery stores or curtain shops for next to nothing. Get creative and wear yours as a belt, necklace, or whatever you wish!

rope belt

appliqué bag detail

quilted bag

Warm gray is a key color feature for many Armani accessories and, wonderfully, this color can be found in many shops at great prices. You can spend a little and still look a million dollars.

A trip to a notions store can instantly bring that Armani magic to any outfit. Look for dull silver or pearlized appliqué motifs—simple florals and geometric designs are a signature look. Just glue a badge pin to the back.

"Timeless,
ageless,
and utterly
desirable"

Mr. Armani does some amazing full-length gowns that grace red carpets across the globe, but for evening glamour he's probably better known for his supersexy cocktail wear. A simple short-sleeved or strapless silver tulip-shaped cocktail dress embodies his understanding of what makes for sophistication and minimal elegance.

Cocktail CHIC

Once you've found this petite girl's must-have, it's all about accessorizing it in the right way to add an air of luxe and to seriously maximize the potential of your cocktail dress.

This is the one time an Armani-esque dress should be above the knee, and if you've got stems to die for, you might as well flaunt them. For added wow and amazing leg-lengthening magic, some superhigh strappy heels are an essential buy. The fact that your leg is on show from above the knee right down to your tootsies will add extra inches to your height. Alternatively, a pair of opaque black tights and some high pumps will look sensational.

The tulip shape of this dress is incredible for creating flattering womanly curves, especially for boyish petite figures—so stand proud and work it! An oversized bangle is the one large piece of jewelry a petite lady can carry off, since instead of swamping you, its large size gives you a great fashion edge.

metallic belt

A metallic belt is a useful tool in any wardrobe and adds an interesting evening twist to any outfit. For an extra edge it's time to get out the toupee tape and ribbon. Simply stick a line of the same black ribbon used for the rosette underneath the belt.

oversized pin

Get your fashion-savvy fingers on a minimally styled pin—a single stone works perfectly. Now add to this by creating a rosette of stiff black ribbon at the back and attach your new creation to the front of the dress.

vintage bag

If you're lucky enough to find a vintage bag at a reasonable price, buy now or regret forever. You'll be dragging it out for all occasions, and it'll never date. If you haven't been lucky enough to find one of these gems, it's not too late. Vintage-style bags have been reproduced and replicated absolutely everywhere.

"Flattering womanly curves: stand proud and work it!"

The fitted mandarin-collar jacket is synonymous with each and every Armani range of clothing. It's a style that's turned into a true classic and is a really worthwhile investment for any age, shape, or size. Make sure it finishes at your hips. Although a longer line may be tempting because it covers your derriere, it can go from incredibly chic to incredibly aging in a flash.

Fitted

CHIC

Try to find a fairly structured fabric with a slight sheen for that extra Armani edge. The fitted style of the jacket will certainly show off a waist, but to make it just a touch more flattering, experiment with a darker waist belt underneath.

Team the jacket with heavyweight linen, wide-leg pants for serious Italian elegance. As we know, wide-leg pants are just the ticket for curvy girls, especially when your bottom is on show. It's imperative that you have the same width at the bottom of your leg as at the top, so make sure there isn't even the hint of a taper in your pants. Texture combinations and subtle tonal changes are what Armani's all about, so off-white linen pants work perfectly here.

cummerbund

Continue the minimal theme around your waist. A steel gray satin belt or cummerbund is great for accentuating a waistline and because it's relatively broad, it is also useful for disguising a tummy.

tote bag

Layered sequins are periodically seen in Giorgio Armani's collections, so an oversized sequin tote bag fits in perfectly. Use a large metallic cocktail ring in a matching hue for an added touch of class. Loving that perfectly styled look.

flat embellished sandal

Giorgio Armani is one of the few designers who allows dressy outfits to be styled up with flat shoes, but this certainly doesn't detract from the glamour. A flat, embellished sandal is completely elegant, and comfortable, too. Just make sure the embellishment matches your belt and bag for a catwalk-worthy look.

"Wide-leg pants are just the ticket for curvy ladies"

If you're not entirely happy with your figure it's always tempting to wear oversized clothing. You may feel it's hiding a multitude of sins, but actually it's piling on the pounds. Something fitted or tailored—but not tight— will show off your best parts, allowing you to be your fabulous self. And watch out for...

SLIMMING TIPS

HORIZONTAL LINES

We all know horizontal stripes aren't the most flattering pattern, but what we sometimes forget is that horizontal lines can be created by using the wrong accessories. For example, a choker on a short neck will add visual pounds and make you look squat, while ankle straps can turn those beautiful ankles into cankles.

PRINTS

Bold graphic prints are really not for everyone, no matter how great they look on the hanger. If you have a fuller figure, bold patterns will draw attention to your upper body and add a dress size. If you're on the petite side, bold patterns could make you look even shorter. My advice is don't write them off, but do experiment and be cautious.

THE RIGHT SIZE

You know that I'm all for embracing your shape, but you also have to embrace your size. Don't be embarrassed when in some shops you're a 10 and in others you're a 12; just head back to the fitting rooms and laugh it off. It may sound obvious, but buy clothes that fit and they will be more flattering; nobody wants to see a roll of tummy hanging over a waistband.

UNDERWEAR

Always invest in good underwear; it can hide a multitude of wobbles. Have one great black, white, and nude-colored set.

HELP!

Get help with showing off that shape! Try a waist belt to highlight your middle. Wear heels when you can—they add height, sexiness, and lengthen stems in a flash. Invest in some tailoring: a tailored pencil skirt can turn a larger bottom into delicious curves, while a one-button tailored jacket can make even the most apple-shaped lady into a voluptuous vixen.

Go for boot-cut-style denims in a darker shade; these help balance out your hips. Alternatively, a pair of skinnies worn with some chunky boots will work in the exactly same way as a pair of boot-cuts. They add visual weight to the bottom of your figure to balance out your overall shape and create a streamlined effect.

The all-in-one «suck me in» bodysuit works wonders.

Red accessories can detract attention from areas of concern.

Pretty red shoes are instant mood lifters and add height, femininity, and glamour.

An LBD with long sleeves can be the answer to the more mature ladies' prayers.

From sports style to perfectly preppy, the American classic look can only be attributed to the über-cool Ralph Lauren. Top fashion tip: it's pronounced how it's spelled and NOT "Laurenne" with a French twist. Apparently he doesn't like it when people say it wrong…

Get the look

Lauren is known around the globe for that all-American clean-cut look and his brilliance in mixing smart and casual pieces together. He often combines items that at first sight don't match, but when they come together on his runway new trends are born.

It all started in 1967 with a range of neckties, and from that he's created an empire of menswear, womenswear, children's wear, and even homewares. He's also the king of the diffusion line with his Gold Label, Black Label, and Lauren ranges, to name a few. And there's no forgetting his Polo line and those renowned, brightly colored polo shirts and sweaters. It's astonishing to think that he had no formal design training, though he did attend a business school, and maybe that goes some way toward explaining his vision.

Although it's probably what he's best known for, Ralph Lauren is not just about the sports-casual look. His eye for design and his pattern cutting for women are second to none, yet they are surprisingly easily replicated. By taking a few pieces of Americana, such as red, white, and blue; cowboy boots; Navajo Indian jewelry; or preppy jackets, and mixing them with basics, you've got it made.

Beautifully cut fabric.

MEGAN FOX
Ralph Lauren really understands the beauty of fabric and cut and is confident enough to allow his dresses to accessorize the women who wear them. In other words, these simple pieces may look like an ordinary column dress on the hanger, but when slipped on they'll make you look like a million dollars!

DIANE KEATON

This is one of the most easily replicated classic Ralph Lauren looks. If your chest size can take it, as Diane's can, a floor-skimming turtleneck dress is age-appropriate and surprisingly sexy. A fine-knit turtleneck sweater and a full-length skirt can be a great replacement for this rather expensive and hard-to-come-by dress.

Simple, elegant silhouette.

varsity stripe with a twist.

JOELY RICHARDSON

Joely's classic Ralph Lauren gown brings together the famous varsity stripe and rosette trend with a glamorous evening look. The vertical stripes are a fabulous figure-fixer and the fishtail bottom of the dress is old-fashioned Hollywood glamour. Chic, timeless, and Americana at its best.

"Make sure it's floor-skimming and fitted at the waist"

At first glance this outfit gives the impression of covering everything up and being perfect for every age, shape, or size, but the body-hugging top and skirt make it a trickier look to carry off than you might imagine. There's also a danger of plaid looking slightly schoolmarmish, so you have to be honest with yourself and make sure it's age appropriate. The key is a youthful personality, a slender body, and a cool hairstyle.

Classic

LINES

A word of warning: if you're well endowed in the bust department, this look may not be very flattering; a turtleneck is the worst item you could ever wear. Although you may feel that covering up is a good thing, it can actually create a shelf of bosom. This makes you look top-heavy to say the least. If you do have the right figure, a fitted black turtleneck is an incredibly useful wardrobe piece. It may be the one time an investment in cashmere is a necessity, simply because an itchy wool worn so close to your body can be really uncomfortable.

On to the skirt: it must be floor-skimming and extremely fitted at the waist. There should be no gathers whatsoever—you don't want to look like a Scottish hotel bedroom. Make sure it's high-waisted to keep things sexy, and top it off with a thick leather belt to add that youthful, couture edge.

With a statement necklace adorning your neck, an oversized gold cuff is the perfect partner for your wrist.

CHANGE THE LOOK
Turn this classic look into a fabulous, dressed-down "wear anywhere" outfit. Take off all the gold accessories and pop on a statement necklace in a subtle colorway. Keep the black leather belt around your middle and finish off with a dark denim jacket and a pair of classic cowboy boots.

The American Classic look is all about natural fibers, so cotton and linen play a huge part, especially during the spring and summer seasons. Always try to find linen that incorporates a small percentage of man-made fiber; this lengthens its life, not to mention minimizing creasing, and, best of all, makes for easier ironing.

Safari CLASSIC

A linen safari-style jacket is a great buy for all ages and sizes, and you've got to love what it does for you. It looks super-stylish, its sleeves cover your arms, and the cut of the jacket nips you in at the waist and accentuates your slenderness even further with its belt detailing. In addition, its length glides over the top of your tummy, streamlining and slimming everything it touches.

Obviously boot-cut jeans are fabulous at elongating any figure, but the trick is to choose your color carefully. Here, I've opted for a natural-colored safari jacket and dark boot-cuts. This is because my model is proud of her upper half and would rather show off that than anything else. If, on the other hand, you're self-conscious about your upper half, go for darker shades up top and keep it light down below.

For daytime cool an oversized, fringed bag is a great way to introduce a hint of Western chic without it looking like a costume. Come nighttime, try changing this for a tan or silver clutch, keeping it big to make you look smaller.

turquoise necklace

Turquoise stones are the perfect color accent for these neutral hues, and they instantly introduce that Navajo vibe, a real signature look for Ralph.

leather belt

How about replacing the self-colored belt of the safari jacket? Woven leather looks fabulous and has an air of the luxury leather brand Bottega Veneta. Another option is a belt with a silver and turquoise buckle for a Western feel.

fringed bag

"The cut of the jacket nips you in at the waist"

This is one of my favorite daytime Ralph Lauren looks and one that's instantly recognizable as preppy American Classic. The key ingredient is a good pair of jeans. A skinny jean will undoubtedly give your look a more youthful edge, but if you are curvier or more mature, a boot-cut jean also looks great. You can "summer up" this combo by going for white jeans.

Preppy *CLASSIC*

The red jacket needs to fit to perfection, so smaller ladies should either head to a good petite department, or don't be scared to take a peek at school uniform departments. Some school blazers are a dead ringer for designer styles and a tenth of the price; just get to a tailor to shape the waist.

Another option for getting a great college-style jacket is to check out an auction website. This style is such a classic and has been around for a while, so people are more likely to sell the originals at a bargain price.

Underneath the jacket lies a crisp striped shirt, and it's an essential; make sure it's slim-fit and ultra-flattering. Remember that you can always revive an old white collar by presoaking it in a solution of warm water and oxygen bleach before washing.

You need to add some authenticity to a blazer in the form of a school or college badge, which can usually be ironed on quickly. Another option is a rosette, but keep it the small side.

badge

dark jeans

The darker the color, the more flattering the look: this rule applies for every shape. I know that finding the perfect pair of jeans is easier said than done, but when you've done so, it's worth investing in every colorway they come in.

boat shoes

A pair of boat shoes is a great alternative to the usual flat option of a sandal or pump. A patent finish will also add extra life to your shoe and will look as good as new 6 months down the line with a quick wipe-over and some new bright white laces.

"Take a peek
at school
uniform
departments"

"Wear the collar up for First Lady attitude and glamour"

You might think that the mix of a work-style white shirt and a formal skirt is somewhat odd, but when styled together correctly it's a fantastic all-American combo. This Oscar-worthy look suits any age, but you can keep a youthful edge by making sure your hair is left down with some extra glossy volume.

Evening CLASSIC

A well-cut white shirt is a good investment for a classic wardrobe. I'm not talking about spending a fortune on designer names, but try a mid-range shirt specialist to keep it looking sleek and chic. A top styling tip is to wear that collar up (try stiffening it with starch) for First Lady attitude and glamour.

Go to a classic eveningwear department for this metallic must-have skirt. It needs to hit the floor, nip you in at the waist, and be double layered. This allows the inner layer to cling while the outer layer sashays over your hips, giving you a to-die-for silhouette.

To tie in with the skirt, keep with a metallic theme for the shoes and don't be tempted to go with a heavy black shoe to match the black accessories; it can ruin the balance of the outfit. Your silver shoe should be strappy, barely there, and comfortably high.

The natural quality of iridescent shell looks effortlessly chic and literally goes with everything. This necklace is amazing for dressing up an evening outfit, but looks equally beautiful with a white shirt and denims for a more laid-back outfit.

shell necklace

black clutch bag

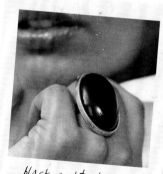

black cocktail ring

For this chic look a satin clutch is the perfect bag. The idea is to keep it simple so as to not to overpower the look, allowing the colors, lines, and silhouettes to make the statement.

It's all about simplicity, so limit yourself to two items of jewelry. Either choose a bracelet with black stones or, my favorite, a jet-black oversized cocktail ring, to complement the necklace.

Ralph Lauren has become synonymous with simple designs and beautifully crafted shapes. His glamorous column dresses and his divine fabric choices allow a woman's body to do the talking, but in the most sophisticated of ways. Either go for a fabric cut on the bias or for a more weighty (sequin-embellished) fabric that hangs and contours in all the right places.

Sexy CLASSIC

Let's start on the inside; it's either all or nothing here, literally! Underwear should be kept to a bare minimum if your figure allows (may I even suggest you go commando?), or the whole kit and caboodle of hold-in tights, hold-in panties, and an uplifting bodysuit and bra combo. Either way, you need the perfect underlying silhouette; that means no lumps, bumps, or lines.

There are two main features for this American Classic look, the dress and you. Let's begin with you. It doesn't matter how much time you spend in front of the mirror, the most important thing is looking fresh and natural, but always with a glossy edge. Keep makeup looking barely there, with soft and subtle hues and delicate golden shimmers.

On to the dress: by all means go for a low-priced version here, but write off a small amount of extra money to have it tailored to fit your body perfectly.

Make sure the shoes match your frock perfectly, and keep the heel superhigh. An open toe is usually more elegant with a long gown—just don't forget to French-manicure those toes.

statement earrings

As with many American classic outfits, a necklace is a definite no-no, but statement earrings are a definite yes-yes. Go with an ethnic pair to contrast dramatically with the red-carpet glamour of the dress.

leather belt

Once again it's all about contrast, and a leather belt is the perfect way to add interest to a simple dress. Go for the equestrian vibe of leather and chain, or go ethnic with an oversized buckle and a splash of color. Either one turns a classic dress into a runway must-have.

open-toe shoes

"Keep makeup looking barely there, with soft, subtle hues"

Jeans are a wardrobe staple for most women (and men), but finding the perfect pair can be trying. Here's what to watch for when shopping for denim.

DENIM RULES

COLOR

The darker the denim, the more flattering the look. In exactly the same way as a completely black outfit will be much more slimming than a completely white outfit, a deep dark indigo is more flattering than a pale wash finish.

Beware of the faded look—this can pile on the visual pounds. Faded areas on the bottom and thighs can accentuate problem areas and are to be avoided at all costs.

POCKETS

No back pockets will only enhance your derriere further. There's a trend at the moment to delete pockets from stretch denims. If you want a J-Lo-inspired booty, then this is the way to go! If, on the other hand, you want to downsize your backside, pockets are absolutely essential.

SIZE

Muffin tops are an unacceptable fashion faux pas. Unfortunately they have become more prevalent with the increase of low-rise denims and high-rise tops. Whatever you do, ignore the sizing and go for what fits; you can always cut out the label.

STRETCH

Remember that denims don't shrink, they tend to get looser. Most denims nowadays have been preshrunk, and some also include a certain amount of stretch fiber. So when trying on, allow for a certain amount of give. Within an hour of wearing, they are likely to feel completely different. A snug fit in the dressing room equals a perfect fit ever after.

Denim with a small amount of stretch is always the most flattering, so look for a little Lycra® in the fiber content. The stretch it creates can make the world of difference and helps smooth out those curves, while doing a marvelous job of holding in any wobbly bits.

LENGTH

Always buy the correct length, $\frac{1}{4}$ in. (5 mm) from the floor. Ankle swingers or crumpled bottoms are a definite fashion no-no.

When shopping for jeans, it is a good idea to take both heels and flats, and always sit down while you are trying on the jeans. This way you can cover any eventuality and get the most out of your purchase.

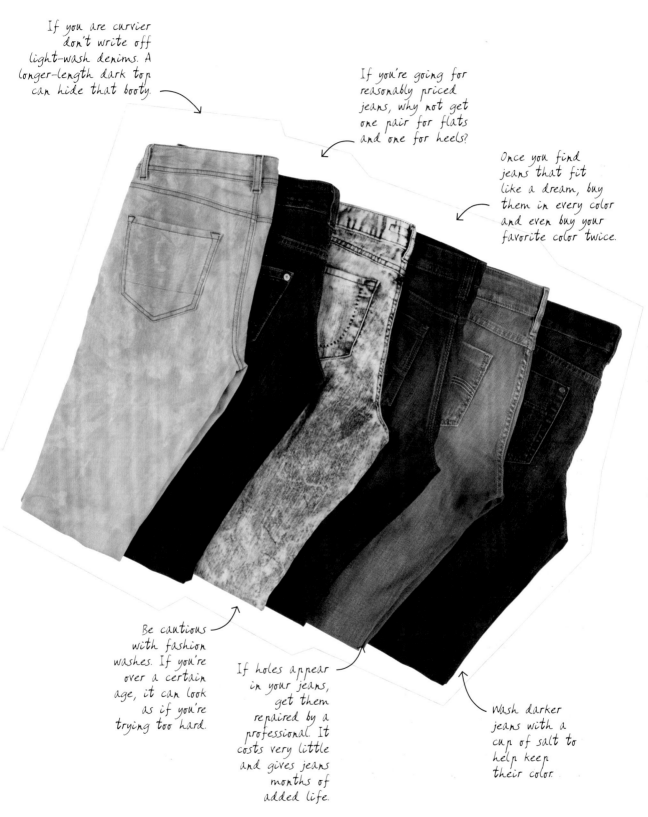

If you are curvier don't write off light-wash denims. A longer-length dark top can hide that booty.

If you're going for reasonably priced jeans, why not get one pair for flats and one for heels?

Once you find jeans that fit like a dream, buy them in every color and even buy your favorite color twice.

Be cautious with fashion washes. If you're over a certain age, it can look as if you're trying too hard.

If holes appear in your jeans, get them repaired by a professional. It costs very little and gives jeans months of added life.

Wash darker jeans with a cup of salt to help keep their color.

THE POWER DRESS

Dress designs come and go, but in 2005 a fashion sensation was born when Roland Mouret launched the Galaxy. It was the dress women had been crying out for: it flaunted their feminine curves, and was ultra-flattering and sensationally sexy. An instant fashion hit, it has left women hungry for more.

Get the look

Celebs the world over couldn't get enough of this design classic, and for once really didn't care if they turned up at an event in the same dress as someone else. No one could part them from their Galaxy (in fact, I'm sure some ended up having them surgically removed). Another plus point for these stunning frocks was how easily they could be changed by adding basic accessories.

Although the cut and design of Roland's masterpiece was second to none, shops across the globe saw the gap in the market for the perfect "dress up or down frock" and replicated the Galaxy left, right, and center. "Inspired by" versions of the famous nipped-in-waist, pencil-length dress can be purchased just about everywhere, and for a fraction of the cost of an original.

Roland Mouret is still going strong, bringing out coveted dress after coveted dress. If you've got the budget, an RM dress is a purchase you'll never regret.

JENNIFER LOPEZ
Jennifer has the perfect body shape for this signature Roland dress. She is oh so proud of her curves and flaunts that bootilicious butt in the most sophisticated and glamorous ways with this much-sought-after RM dress. The white colorway accentuates her ladylike silhouette even further, absolute proof that Mr. Mouret knows how to cut for a woman.

Flaunting those curves.

VICTORIA BECKHAM

A Mouret dress is almost like a uniform for Mrs. Beckham, and this more daring color choice has really paid off. Her superskinny figure is actually enhanced by this to-die-for frock. It's not that it adds pounds, but it gives the illusion of a more a voluptuous physique. Faultless and fabulous.

The perfect LBD.

Figure-enhancing cut.

Chic and demure.

CAMERON DIAZ

I always say it—when you find the perfect LBD it will never be off your back. This divine little number looks amazing either on its own or, as Cameron wears it, styled up with some statement shoes. Whether it's a bona fide Galaxy or something that looks fairly similar, the versatility of this wardrobe must-have is endless.

"This look will set you apart in the workplace"

The sleek nature of this frock simply oozes sophistication and style, yet it is still incredibly wearable. The capped sleeves are a great way of showing some skin, yet not showing your upper arms if you're self-conscious about them. This shorter version is great if you're proud of your stems.

Dress for
WORK

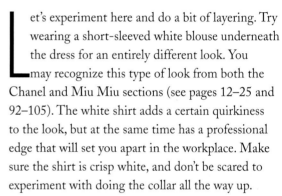

Let's experiment here and do a bit of layering. Try wearing a short-sleeved white blouse underneath the dress for an entirely different look. You may recognize this type of look from both the Chanel and Miu Miu sections (see pages 12–25 and 92–105). The white shirt adds a certain quirkiness to the look, but at the same time has a professional edge that will set you apart in the workplace. Make sure the shirt is crisp white, and don't be scared to experiment with doing the collar all the way up.

Layer a selection of pearl strands over the top, but watch out for supersize—anything too big may be fashion overkill. Try wearing a simple black patent leather pump and matching belt for optimum professional style.

CHANGE THE LOOK

Going straight from work to a hot date? No problem. The classic black of this dress will last a lifetime and is just as fabulous in the evening as it is during the day.

Another color that looks amazing no matter what age you are is gold. Accentuate your womanly curves by drawing attention to what will naturally be your narrowest part. Don't overdo the belt here; as with so many accessories, you need to keep details to a minimum. A simple, thick gold band will do the job perfectly. Continuing on this theme, keep the clutch bag as simple as can be. If your statement necklace has a matching bangle, then wear it with pride. Last but not least, let's talk shoes: go for it and choose high, sexy, gold stilettos.

A black Roland Mouret-style dress should be a curvy girl's best friend. The body-hugging shape clings to your womanly physique and flaunts that sexy silhouette to perfection. At the same time your upper arms stay covered and the knee length cut keeps chunky legs under wraps at all times—what more could you ask for?

Dress for a WEDDING

Keep the lines and shapes clean and simple and go monochrome all the way. A vintage-effect faux-fur bolero in ivory will look amazing and completely change the feel of the dress. Keep the vintage style going with long strands of pearls that will further elongate your body. Bring attention up top with a fabulous mini-hat fascinator. Wear this with confidence and toward the front of your head. Create an air of mystery and sophistication by adorning the headpiece with your own black net; it costs next to nothing yet can really add some drama to your outfit.

Team the fascinator with some red lips, and all eyes will be focused on your top half, allowing any lumps and bumps lower down to be kept secret at all times. Finish the look with a cream satin bag and matching on-trend heels.

CHANGE THE LOOK

If you are a curvier girl, layering up isn't always a no-no, but if you're very well endowed in the bust department, this might not work for you. A turtleneck can do terrible things to a larger bosom, so just don't go there.

If, on the other hand, you're in perfect proportion, then layer a fine-knit chocolate-brown turtleneck under your short-sleeved Galaxy-esque dress. The combination of brown and black is style and sophistication personified and is one of my favorite combos.

Continue the chocolate-brown vibe with some 20-denier , and then draw the eye down with some fabulous boots. No matter what shape or finish a boot has, as long as it hits you at the knee it is tremendous for balancing out your figure. The visual weight boots create at the bottom of your body counteracts any weight you may have on your butt, belly, or thighs.

"Accessories
keep all eyes
focused on
your top half"

If you've got the confidence, this is the time to make the most of color. An vivid lilac frock is both fashion-savvy and statement-making. Because it's such a bold hue, if you don't have a naturally slim-line figure, be sure to wear some serious hold-in underwear and flaunt any curves you have with pride.

Dressing
UP COLOR

It's all too easy to dress down bright colors by teaming them with darker neutral shades, but in my opinion this is a real waste. Go for it with some catwalk-worthy color blocking. Fuchsia pink looks incredible with the lilac, and when put together they create a real standout look.

Start up at the top with some vibrant pink earrings, but be careful not to go too plastic, which can completely cheapen the outfit. Also, keep your lips neutral. Matching lips and earrings can look more "girl band" than sassy glamour-puss.

Get yourself a pink waist belt that will further define that fabulous figure, and carry through the pink with an oversized statement ring. When it comes to the bag and shoes, go for either silver or pink satin to keep things looking supersleek.

CHANGE THE LOOK

A summer wedding is the perfect time to flaunt color, and the contrasting hues of coral and lilac are a match made in heaven. The great thing about this color combination is that the purple hue helps cool down red tones in the skin, while coral brightens up even the most sallow of complexions. So anyone can wear this dynamic duo.

Let's begin with this easy-to-wear fascinator. Stick with the coral color, but keep it neat and simple with a single flower that clips into your hair. This allows you to wear your flower as a corsage on another outfit at a later date. Put it on a dress, a jacket, or even a handbag and up the style stakes in a flash.

To continue the color block, go for the cheap and effective option of using a thin metallic belt layered over a colored belt. As far as the finishing touches are concerned, go for metallics. Try a matching satin clutch and some gold strappies to earn maximum style points.

"Go for it with some catwalk-worthy color"

"Create an air of nautical glamour and sophistication"

Navy is a fantastic color choice for a superfitted, supersexy dress. We all know that black is incredibly flattering, but it doesn't suit everyone because it can drain color from many skin tones. A true navy is as dark and as slimming as its moodier counterpart, yet oozes sophistication.

Nautical DRESS

Team this dress with a white one-button blazer, which is great for covering problem arms and really lends something to the outfit. Add some nautical detail with oversized red beads. Try using a red, white, and blue scarf instead of a waist belt; it's a creative and inexpensive option that will get you noticed for all the right reasons.

To add an air of nautical glamour, a red mock-croc bag is the best way to go: make it oversized and balance out your figure at the same time. Whatever you do, don't be temped to go for any anchor motifs; in fact, any seashore details will turn this fashion-forward look into a shipwreck. To round off the outfit, go for some supersexy, vertiginous heels in red patent.

CHANGE THE LOOK

Your must-have navy dress, which hits your knee and clings in all the right places, looks amazing when teamed with black. Obviously the tailoring of the dress is fabulously flattering, but when combined with a one-button tux-style jacket, it just gets better. It gives your outfit some grown-up edginess, but still has an extremely fashion-forward feel.

Don't be scared of mixing these two colors together. Navy and black is a firm fave with many fashion designers. When they're put together they create an air of sophistication that each individual color could never achieve alone.

Add further glamour with jet-black jewelry and a matching navy bag to give this outfit an incredibly luxe edge. On the bottom half, keep it extremely slimming and simple with 40-denier tights and a minimal yet ultra-effective pair of black pumps.

A sleeveless, shapely power dress can be one of the most versatile items you'll ever own. It can be worn to any occasion and can be worth investing a bit of money in. A variety of basic fitted dresses can easily be found in most petite ranges. The smaller the fit, the more fabulous they look, and this makes the world of difference.

Dress in
LAYERS

Part of the dress's versatility is that you can layer items underneath as well as over the top, and an eye-catching red tailored shirt looks amazing. Make sure the shirt is fitted so no excess fabric spoils the lines of the dress. A shirt specialist is probably the best place to go for this item; they'll have all the colors and cuts you'll ever want at really reasonable prices.

Add an extra-feminine touch with a jet-black necklace, and you're on to a winner. Carry through the glossy black color theme and get your hands on a patent leather tote bag. Again, this is über-feminine, but has a definite business edge. Put the icing on the cake with a pair of killer red heels and knock 'em dead in the boardroom.

CHANGE THE LOOK

Don't be shy—it's time to sparkle. This can be done on either a dress that could use a new lease on life, or on a bargain buy that you don't mind getting a bit creative with.

If it's a dress that's seen better days, start by reviving it with a standard washing-machine black dye. This will make your tired old dress look as good as new. Then get down to the notions store and buy some iron-on rhinestone motifs. Stick to one design and simple strips of the same size rhinestones. Now all that's left to do is place them on the fabric and let your iron do the hard work. Before you know it you'll have the dress of your dreams.

Finish your new fashion masterpiece by teaming it with other rhinestone accessories.

"Layer items
underneath
as well as
over the top"

When you're going from office to bar, you need a few quick fixes to set the scene for the evening ahead. With some fashion-forward accessory choices, you can turn your work outfit into a runway replica.

OUTFIT CHANGERS

STATEMENT JEWELRY

Whether it's an in-your-face seasonal piece like an ethnic necklace or a fabulously bold, colored number, these can instantly turn an otherwise straitlaced outfit into a real conversation piece. The same can be said for a statement bracelet or catwalk-worthy chandelier earrings.

METALLIC CLUTCH

Ditch your dull daytime briefcase for an on-trend match-with-anything metallic clutch. It can be silver, pewter, gold, or bronze. Whatever the color, it adds instant glamour and style.

HOSIERY

Changing your black opaque tights for either fun and funky colors or sexy lace can give any outfit that nighttime fashionista edge. Pick the season's ultimate colorway or add an extra air of chic with delicate net or lacy patterns.

UNLAYERING

When you know you're going from work to a date, wear a power dress with layers under and over to the office. Removing these layers turns you from office angel to nighttime glamour-puss in an instant.

SPARKLY SHRUG

Shrugs are an invaluable tool for an evening event and can glam up even a basic cotton tank top, plus they also hide problem arms. They tend not to crease and can be rolled in a ball and kept in the bottom of your bag, literally waiting for the words, "How about going out for a drink?"

STATEMENT HEELS

Hide everyday office flats in the supply closet and get out those head-turning, skyscraper heels. Your confidence and attitude will instantly change and you'll be ready for a night on the town. Don't just add height; bold color with a black outfit can make the world of difference and screams, "Let's party!"

THE LIPSTICK FACTOR

Luscious red lips may not be appropriate for a meeting with Human Resources, but when 5.30 hits, it's time to vamp things up a few notches. Remember, if you don't have any lipstick on hand, stop at a department store and get a free sample.

A waist belt takes up little room in your bag, but immediately adds womanly curves and a sexy edge to your corporate gear.

A metallic bag in a soft color can be worn both to the office and on a night out.

Changing your bag for a clutch adds a party air to any outfit.

Colored shoes are an instant mood lifter and elongate legs when worn with the same-colored hosiery.

Index

Acknowledgments

AUTHOR'S ACKNOWLEDGMENTS

I would like to thank everyone at Octopus Publishing Group for not only believing in me, but for all their help, support and guidance. Thanks to all the shops in Oxford Street, London, especially Debenhams, to Robert and my family for their untold support, and to my right-hand girl Sarah Tankel, who helps me with just about everything, is incredibly talented, creative and hard working, plus an amazing friend and colleague.

OTHER THANKS

Ray Gaddu, Nese Schaffer, Sasha Abraham, Andii Davis, Louise Spears, Emma Pollard, Lorraine Kelly, Michael Joyce, Sarah Castro Pearson, Graham Atkins-Hughes,

PUBLISHER'S ACKNOWLEDGMENTS

Executive Editor **Katy Denny**
Senior Editor **Lisa John**
Executive Art Editor **Penny Stock**
Designer **Miranda Harvey**
Senior Production Controller **Carolin Stransky**

All photography by **Graham Atkins-Hughes** with the exception of the following:

Getty Images Daniele Venturelli/WireImage 30; Evan Agostini 159 right; Gregg DeGuire/WireImage 159 left; James Devaney/WireImage 95 right; Jason Kempin/Film Magic 126; Jon Furniss/WireImage 111 right; Tim Whitby 94

Press Association Images AJM/EMPICS Entertainment 79 right; Chicago/EMPICS Entertainment 31 left; Cosima Scavolini/LaPresse/Empics Entertainment 63 left; David Miller/ABACA USA/Empics Entertainment 62; Doug Peters/EMPICS Entertainment 31 right, 110; Frederic Nebinger/ABACA 14; Graylock/ABACA USA/Empics Entertainment 127 left; Gregorio Binuya/ABACA USA/Empics Entertainment 63 right, 78; Ian West/PA Archive 15 left, 46; Jano/Starmax/EMPICS Entertainment 158; Paul Smith/EMPICS Entertainment 142; Tammie Arroyo/UK Press 79 left

Rex Features Daniele Venturelli 47 right; Gregory Pace/BEI 143 left; Matt Baron/BEI 143 right; Miquel Benitez 15 right; Most Wanted 47 left; Olycom SPA 95 left; Peter Brooker 127 right; Richard Young 111 left